I0505584

Cycles of Europe

Udaybhan Singh

FRONT COVER: Cycle seen in Bratislava

Photographs © Udaybhan Singh

No part of this book may be reproduced, scanned, or distributed in any printed or electronic form without permission of the author.

Book Design by Udaybhan Singh

Copyright © 2015 Udaybhan Singh

All rights reserved.

ISBN: 1508995362
ISBN-13: 978-1508995364

DEDICATION

This book is dedicated to my family – my mom, dad and sister. My MOM Mrs. Santosh, DAD Mr. Hiralal and SISTER Ms. Kirti who have always supported me in pursuing this endeavor. Thank you so much.

ACKNOWLEDGMENTS

I would like to thank my Nikon D5100 and Nikkor lens creators and all those wonderful people who ride these beautiful machines in Europe.

ABOUT THIS ART WORK

Everyone loved cycling when they were kids. I remember when I was a kid my parents had bought a cycle for me and I was very much excited to learn cycling. In the learning phase, my parents ran behind me to ensure that I don't fall. It was fun and soon I was able to ride the entire town myself. It was the best gift a child could get in those days. Remember we did not had Personal Computers, Internet, Mobile phones and Xboxes in those days. So, Cycling was one of the best past time activities back those days. I had my cycle for almost 6 years. Later when I realised that I have grown up we decided to scrap the bicycle. As you grow up you tend to incline towards other fuel powered machines. However, cycles or bikes still hold an important place in the children's lives even today though more as a skillset.

When I was backpacking in Europe I was very much fascinated seeing bicycles in every hook and corner of the street. The fact that people of all ages cycle daily to their work or to the market or just for a leisure ride and the well paved cycling roads adds to the overall cycling culture. As a traveller and an aspiring photographer I could not hold but took my camera out and started capturing these beautiful machines. All the cycles were clicked in their natural settings across following 9 cities in Europe – Warsaw, Krakow, Berlin, Prague, Cesky Krumlov, Budapest, Vienna, Ljubljana and Bratislava.

I wish to capture more of these pictures across every single country in Europe one day.

To keep this Project going I am raising funds by selling Canvas, Matt and Gloss prints of few of these pictures. Any print you order comes with a personalised Thank You note hand written by me. Digital version of this art work can be checked on **https://cyclesofeurope.wordpress.com** or my personal blog **https://udsinghprojects.wordpress.com**

Happy Cycling, Keep Smiling – Future of a better city!

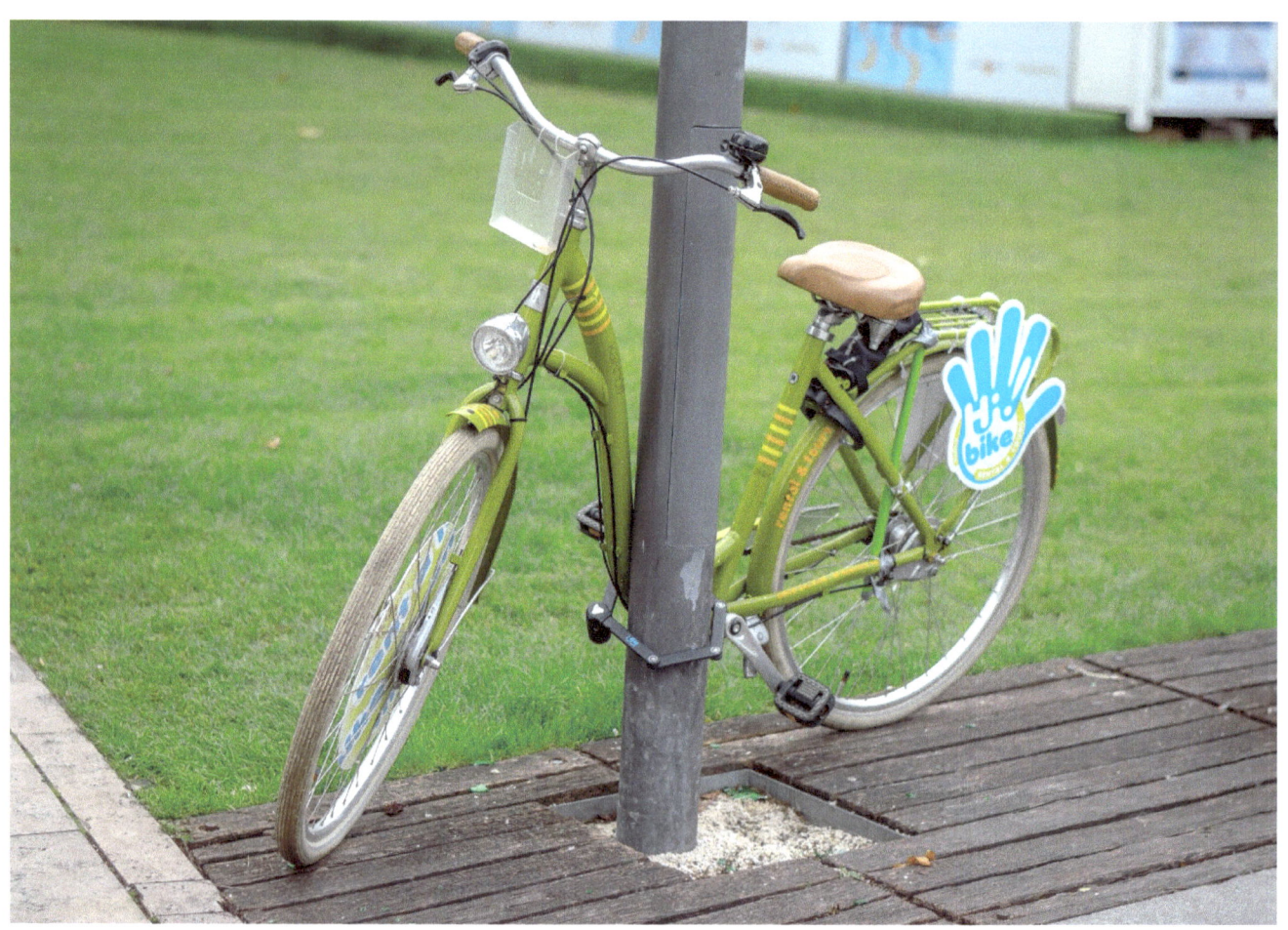

#Seen in Budapest

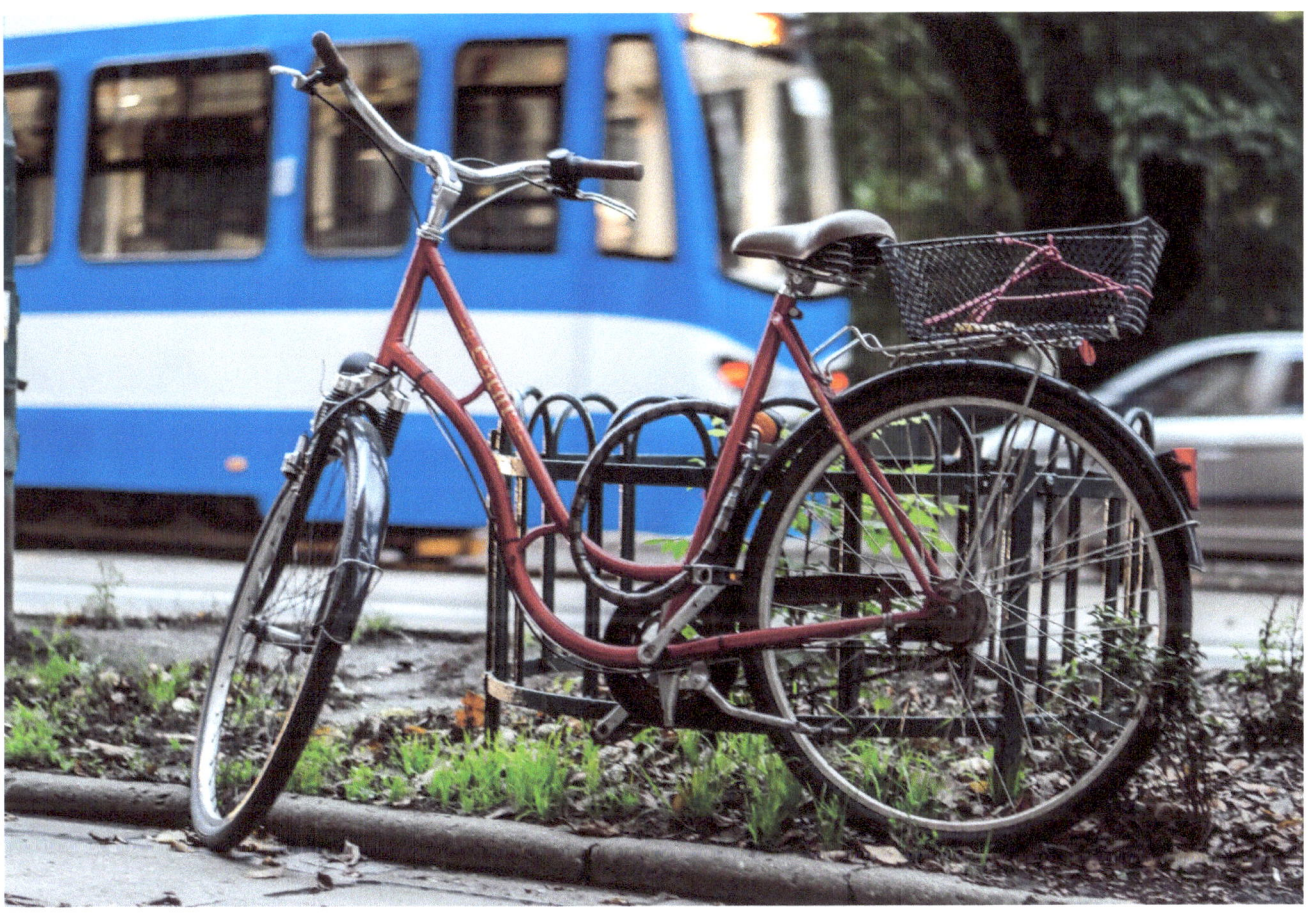

\# Seen in Warsaw

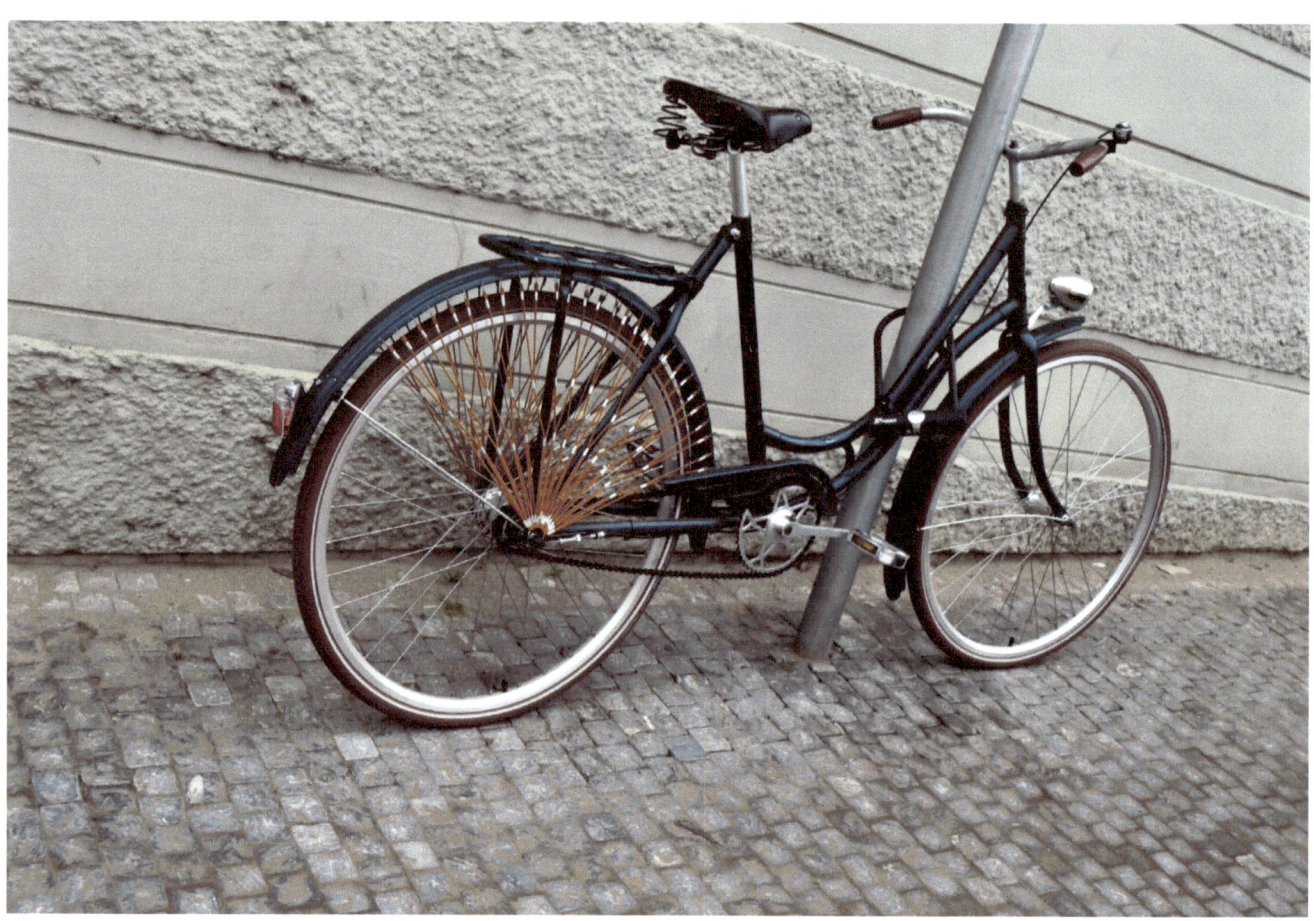

#Seen in Prague

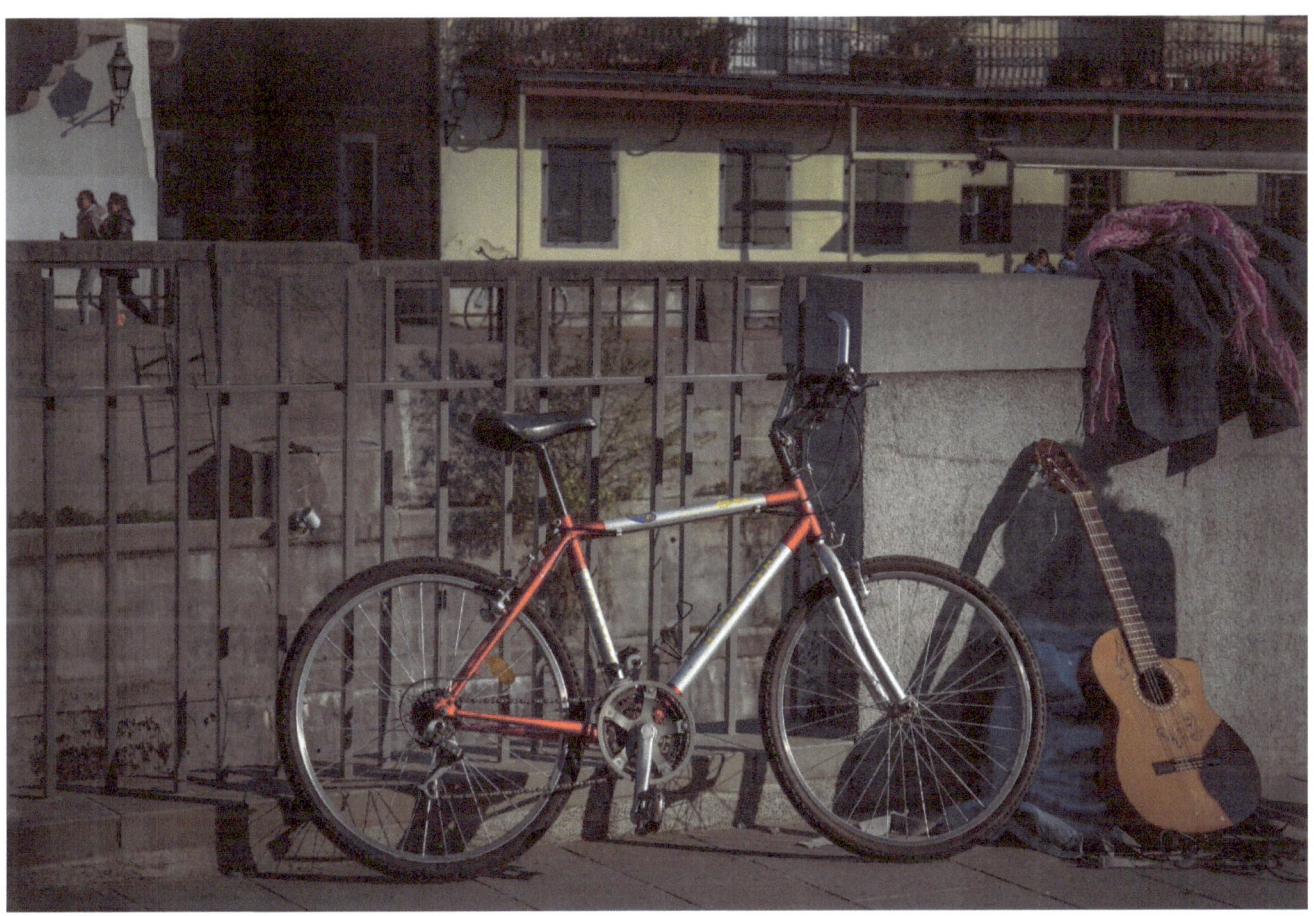

#Seen in Ljubljana

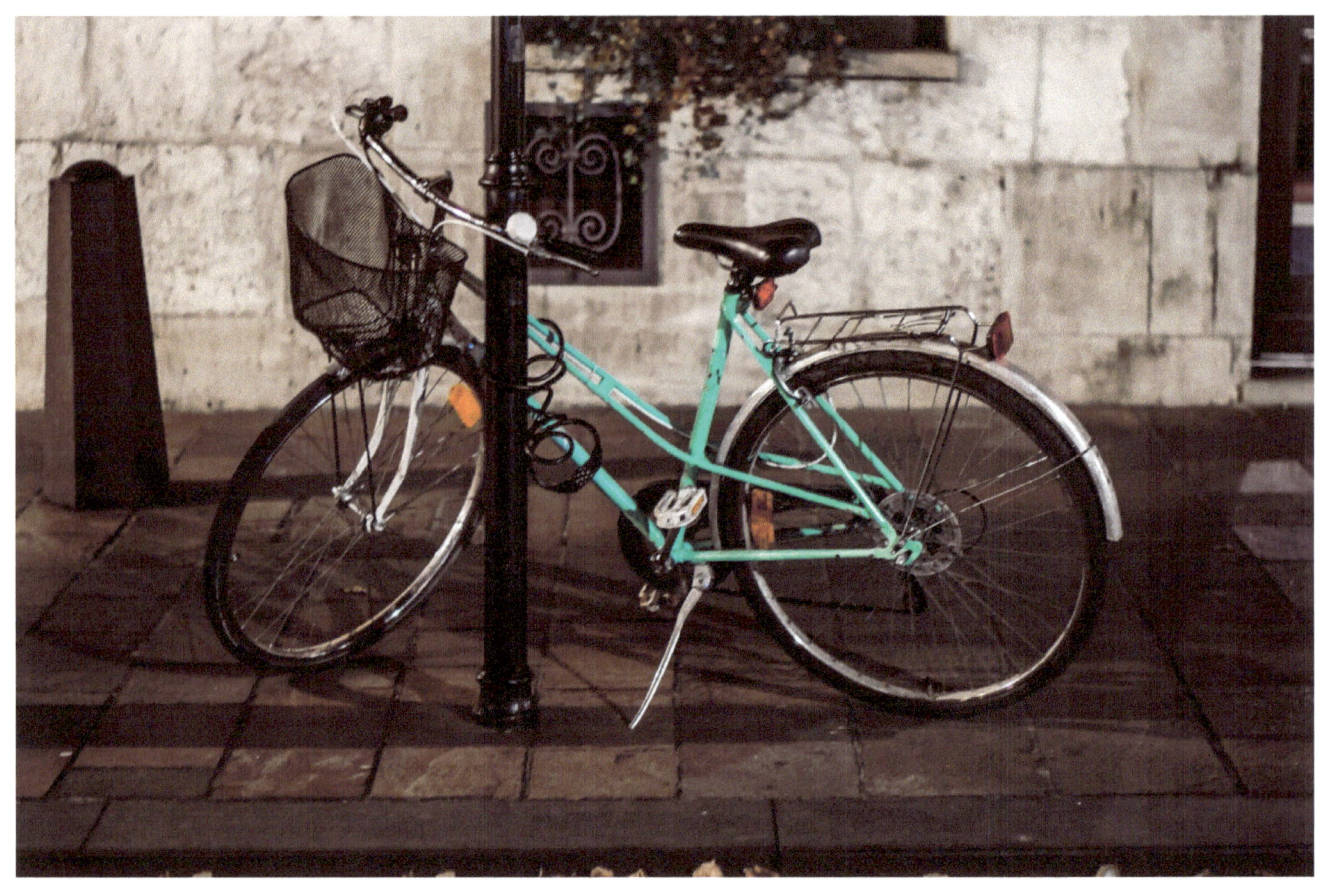

#Seen in Krakow

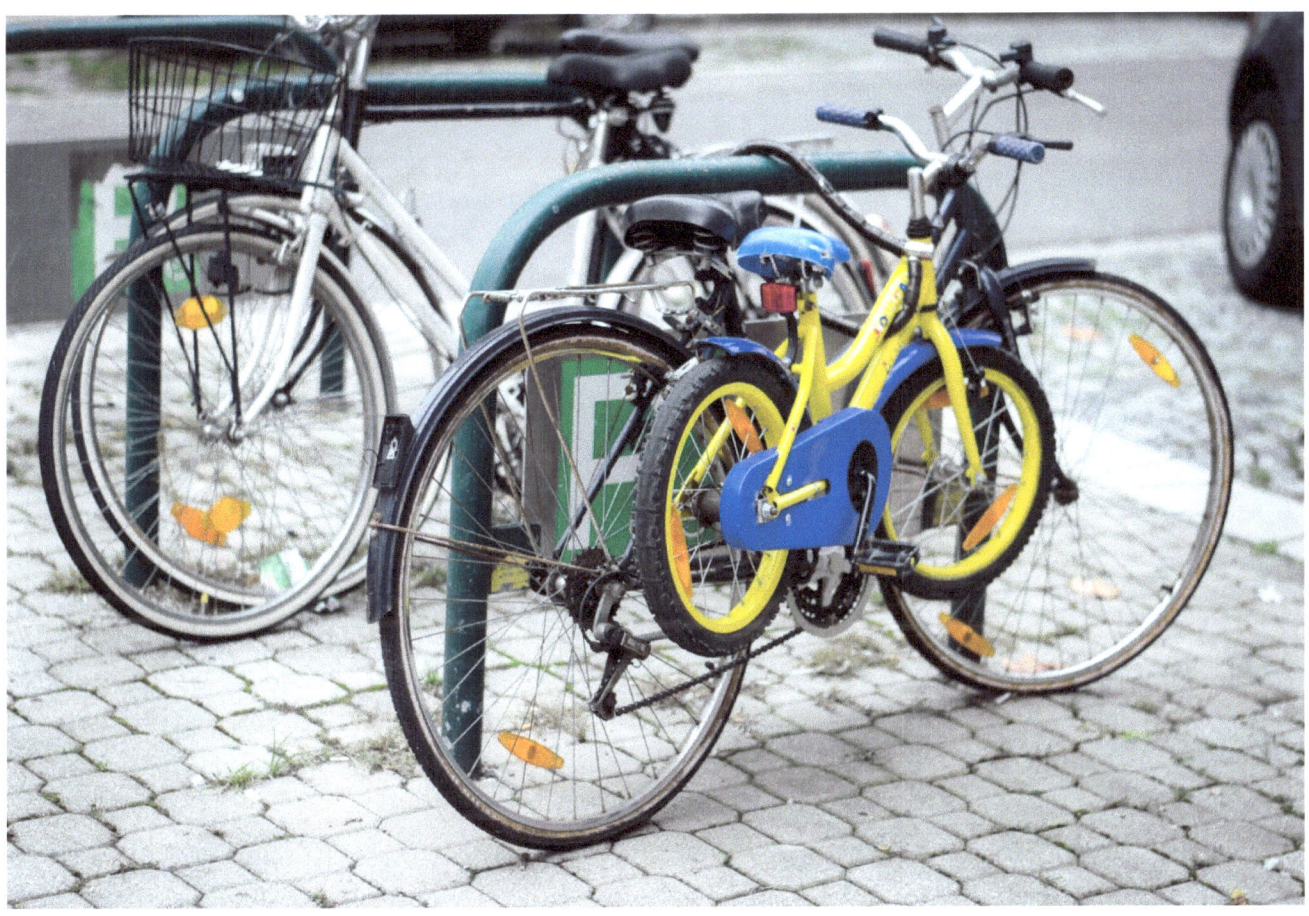

#Seen in Vienna

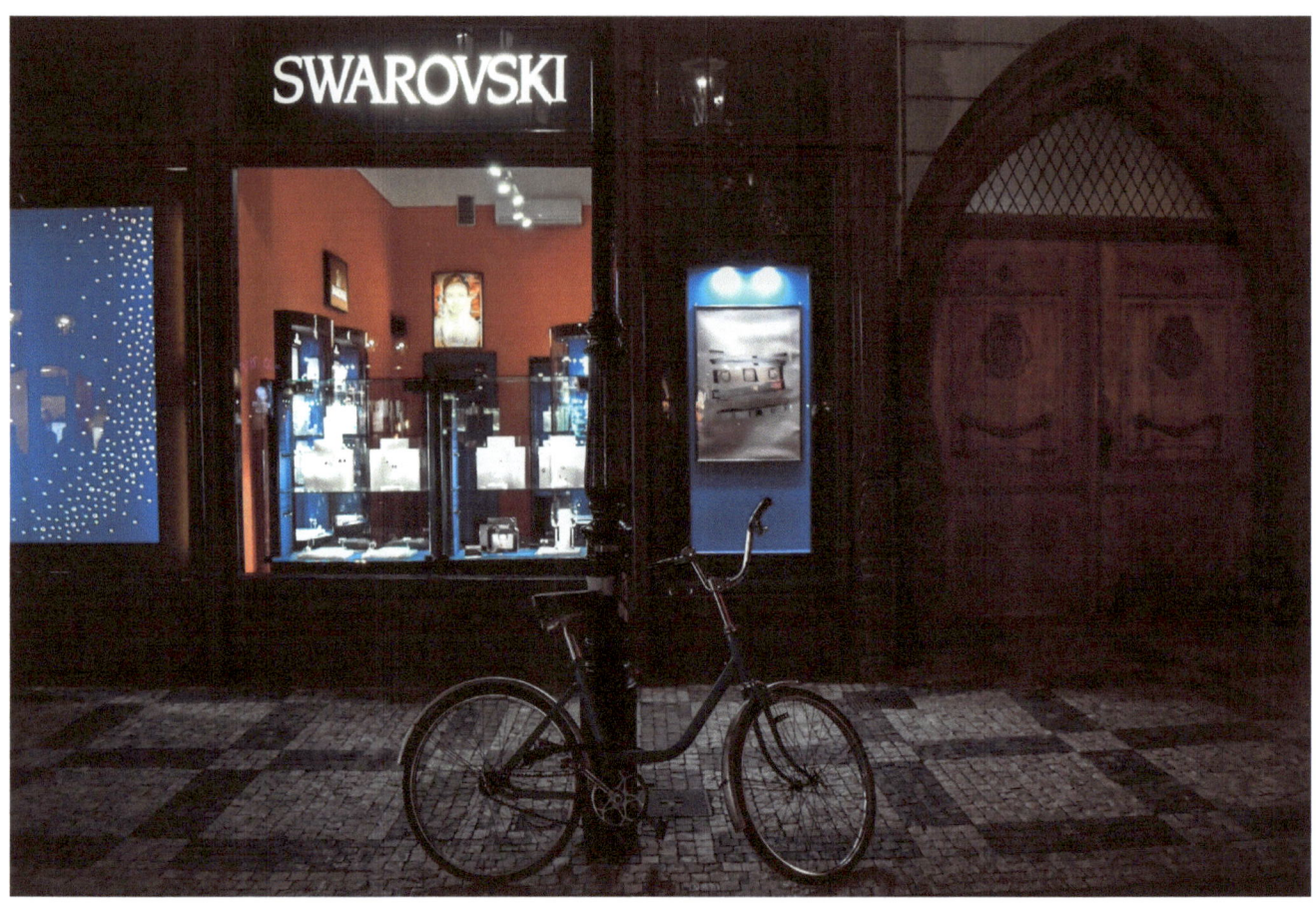

#Seen in Prague

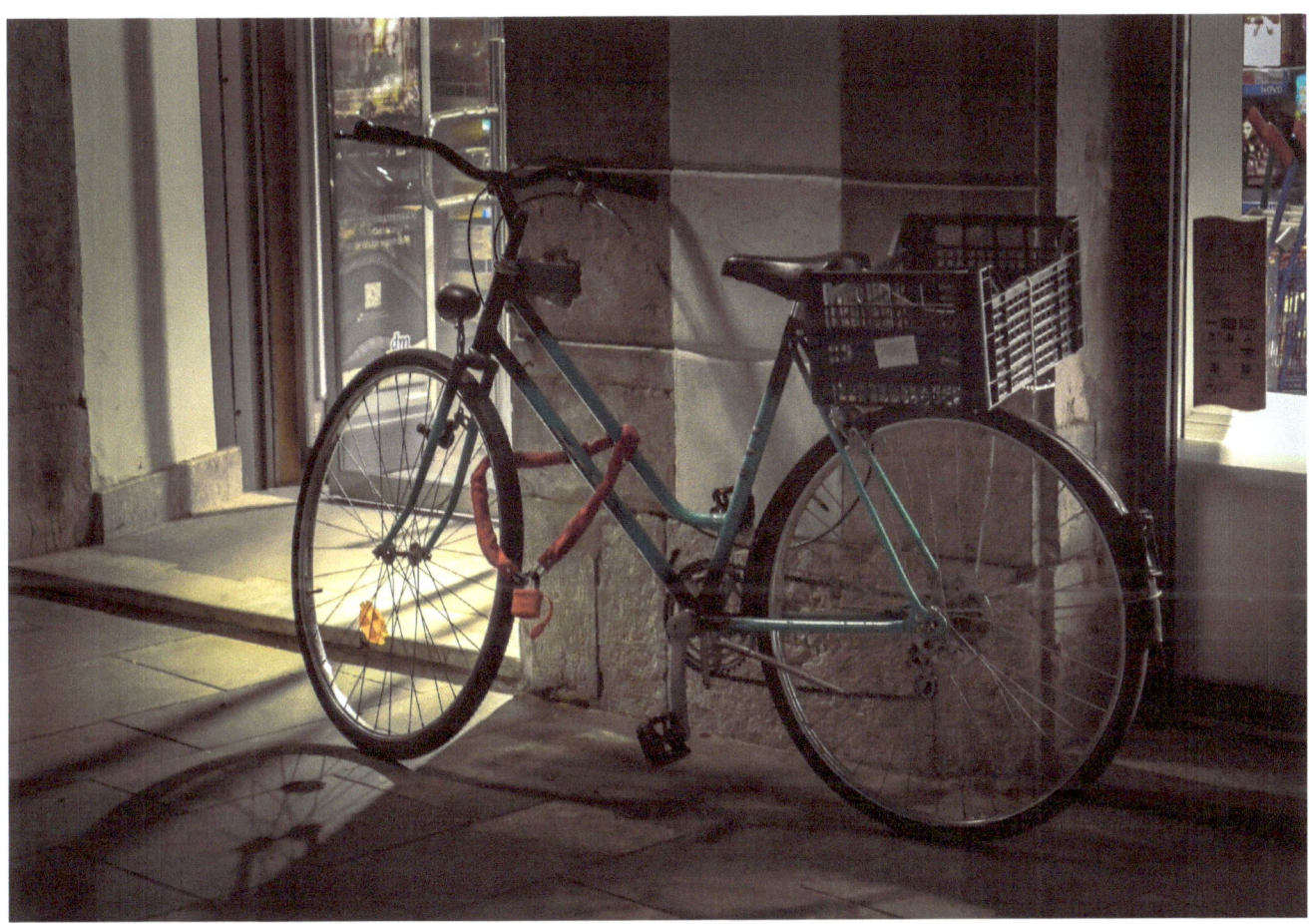

#Seen in Ljubljana

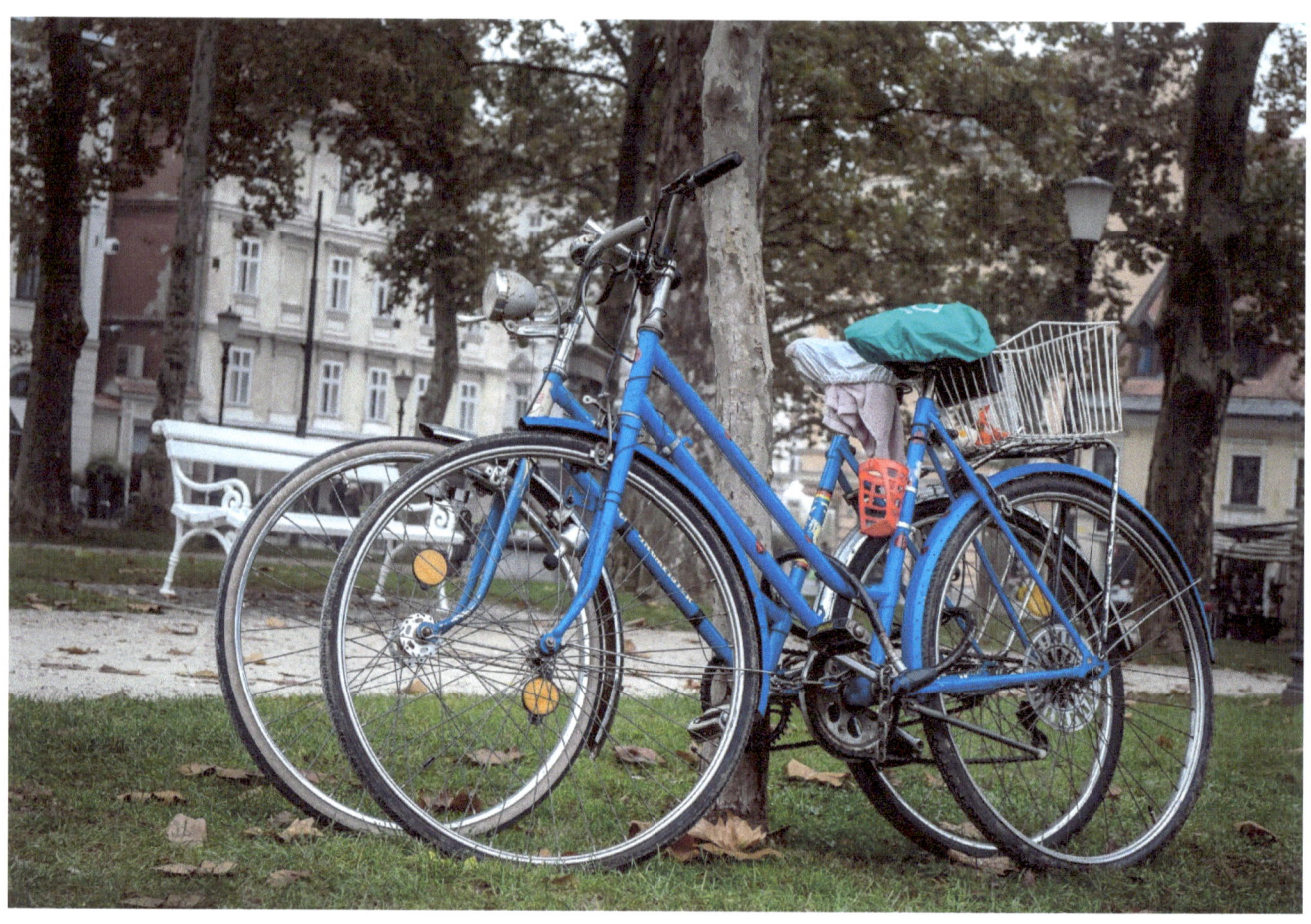

#Seen in Ljubljana

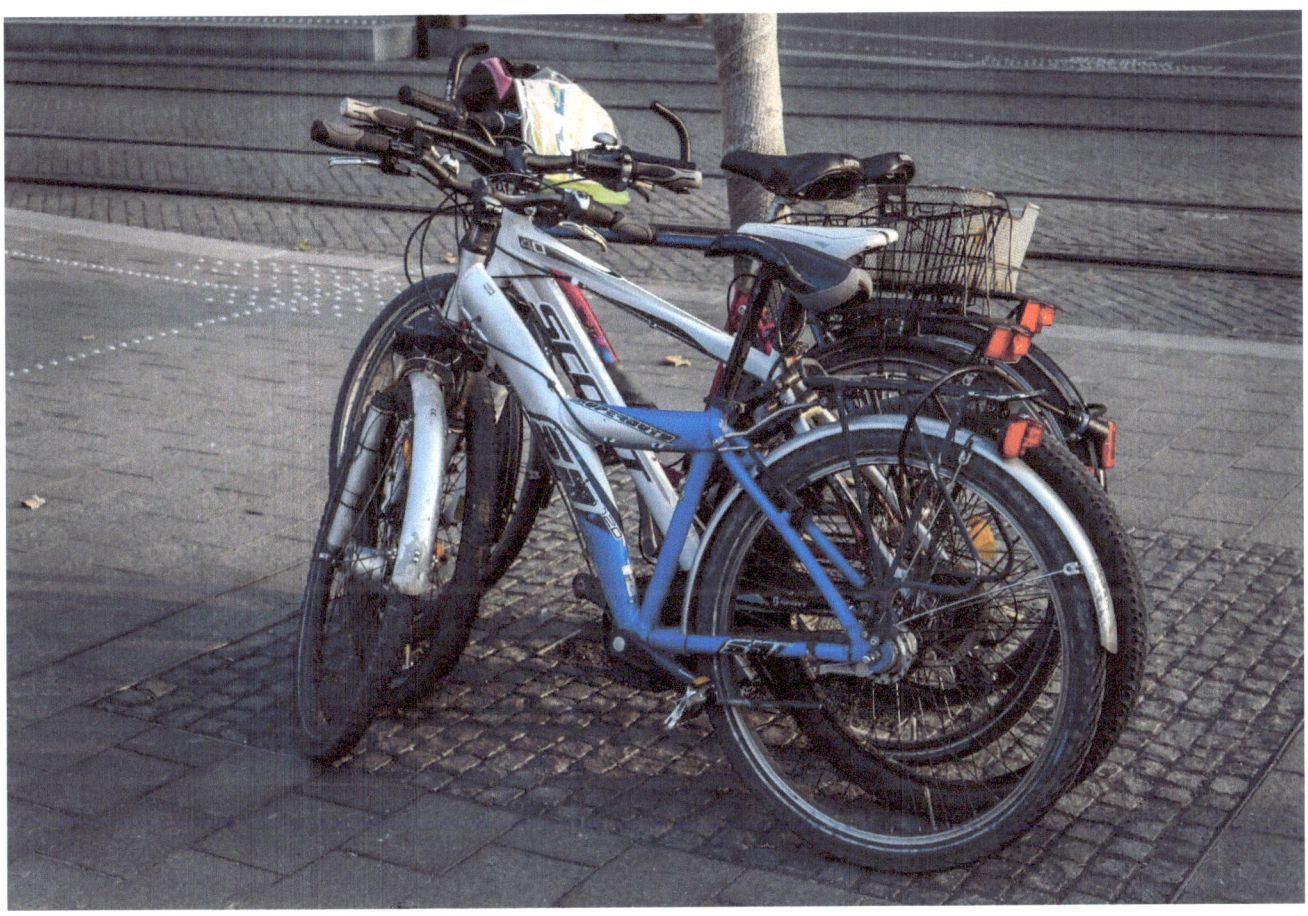

#Seen in Budapest

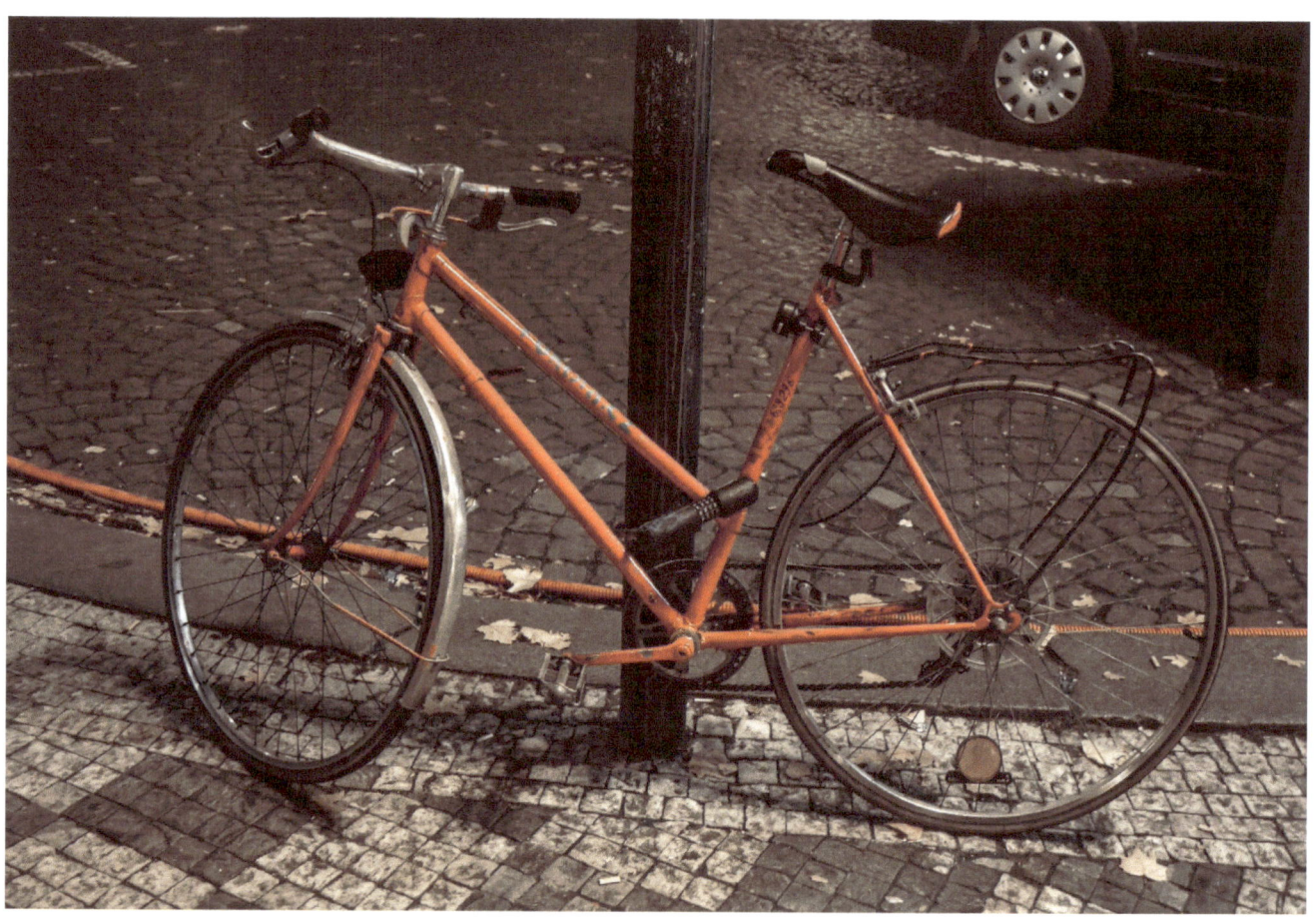

#Seen in Prague

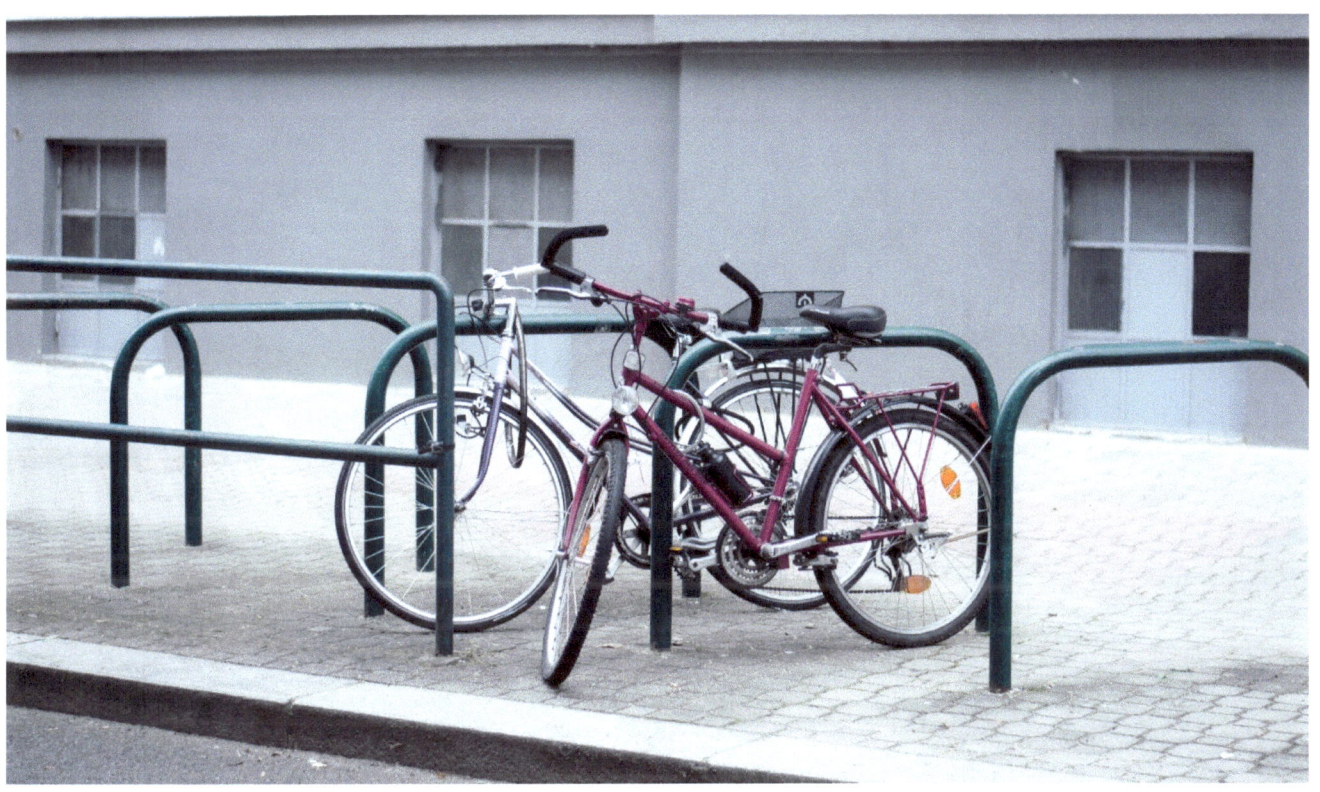

#Seen in Vienna

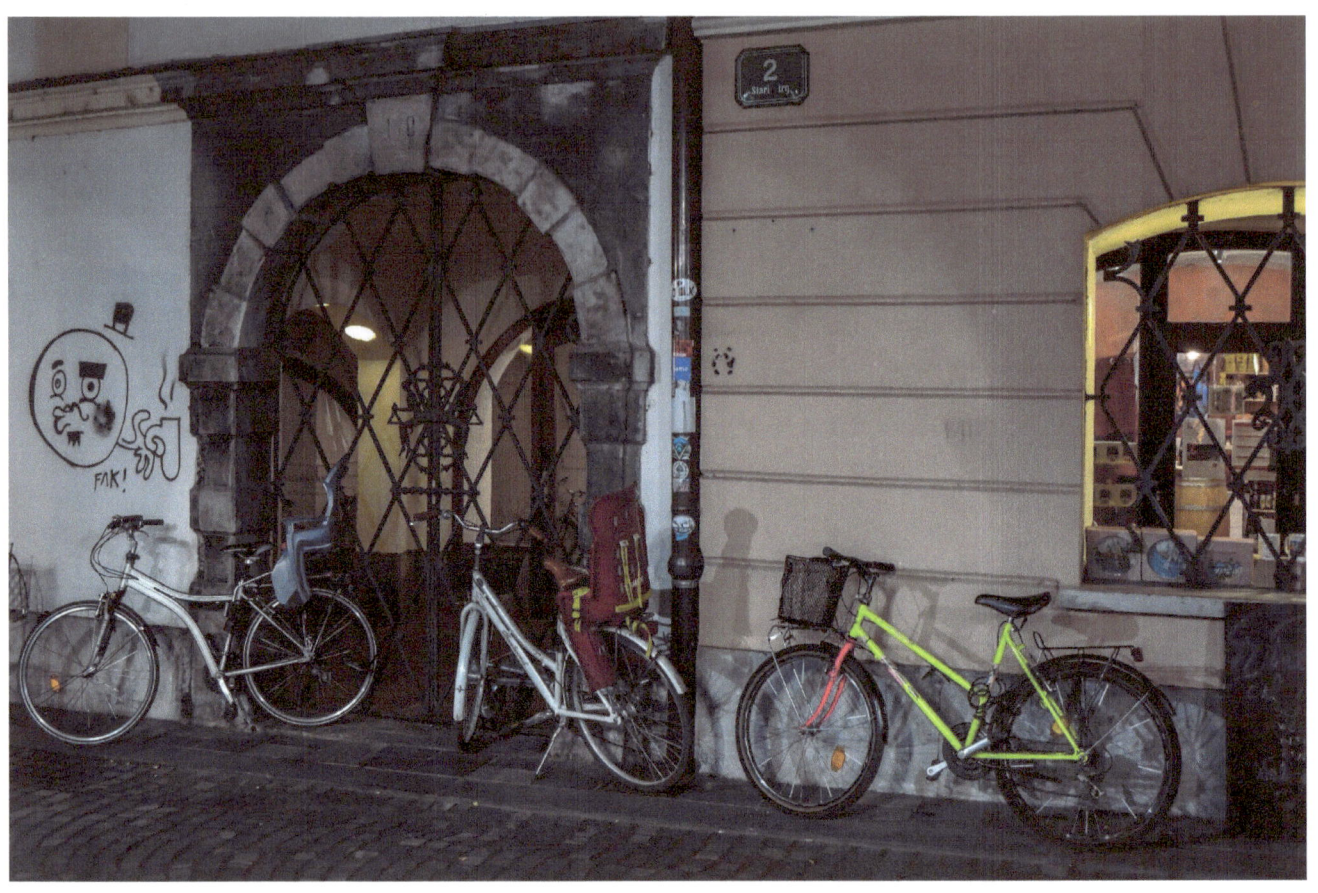

#Seen in Ljubljana

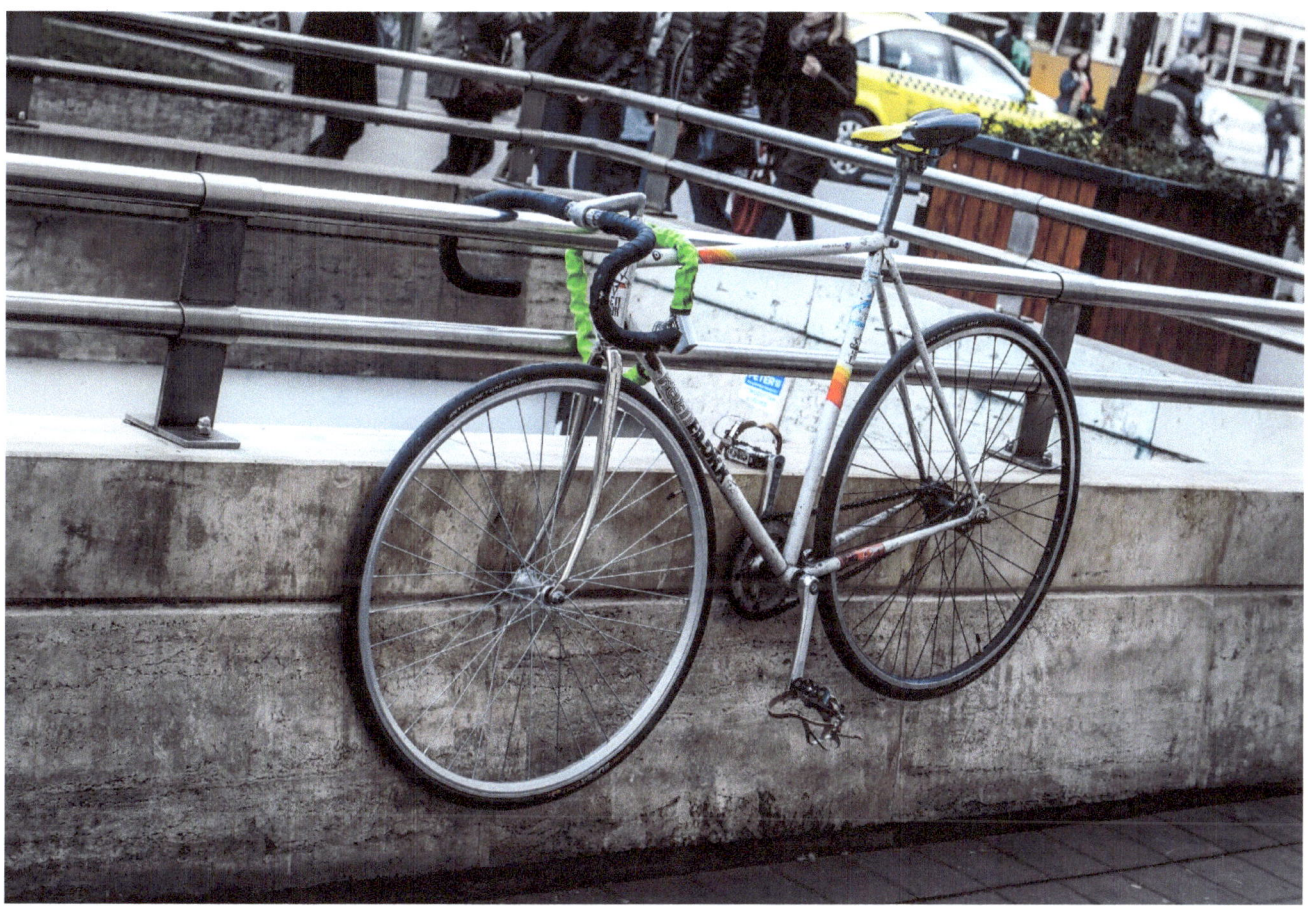

#Seen in Budapest

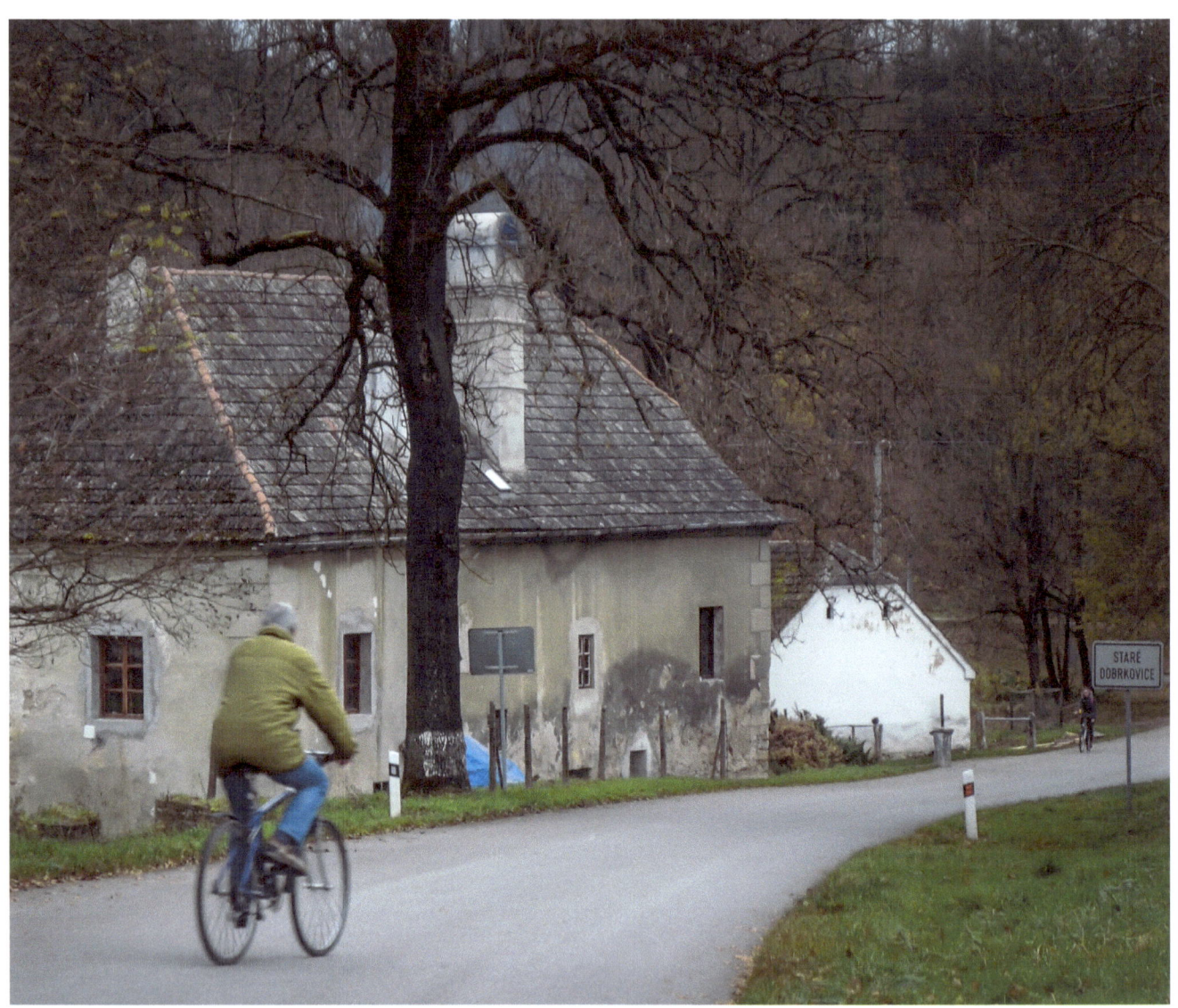

#Seen in Cesky Krumlov

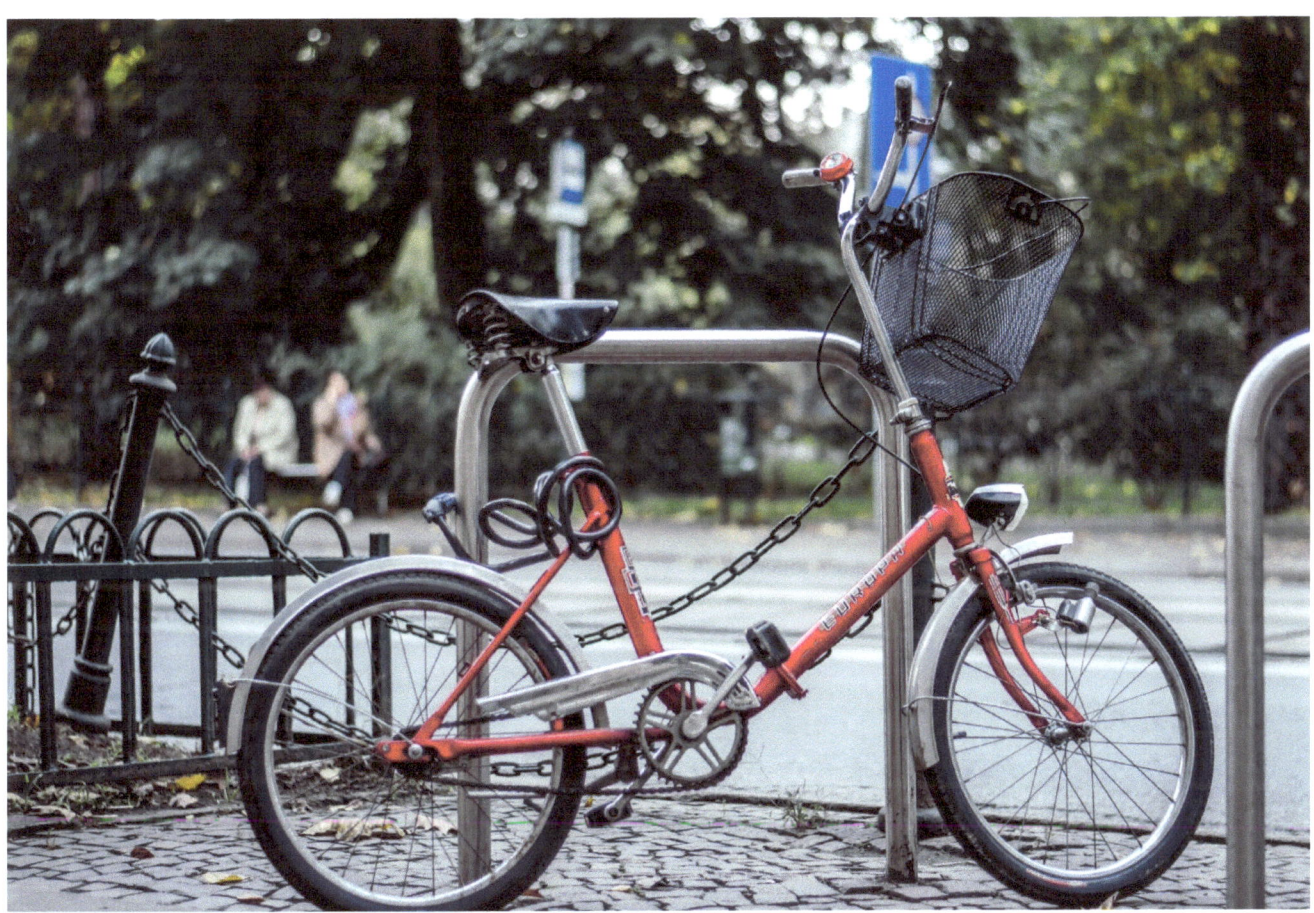

#Seen in Warsaw

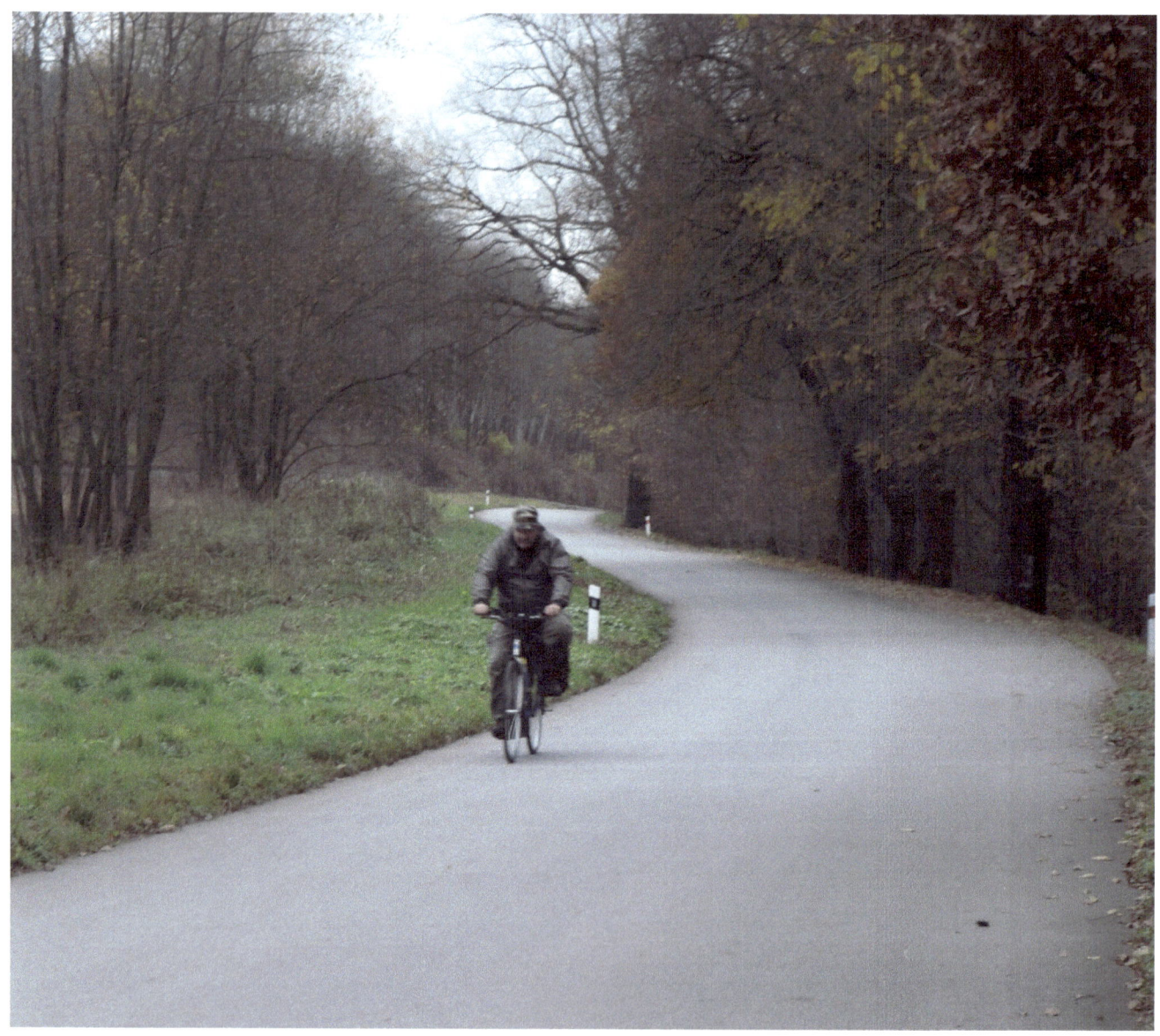

#Seen in Cesky krumlov

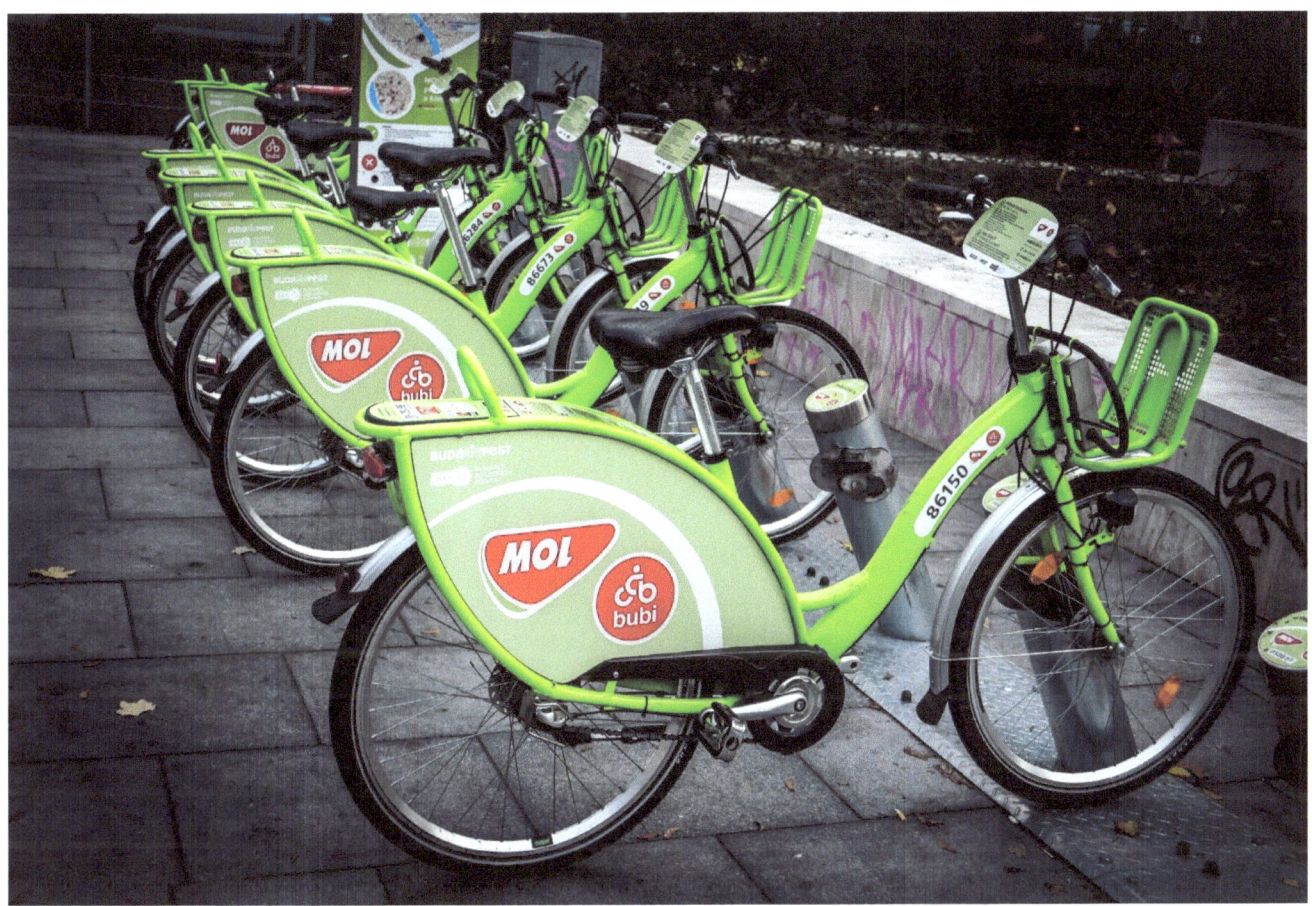

#Seen in Budapest

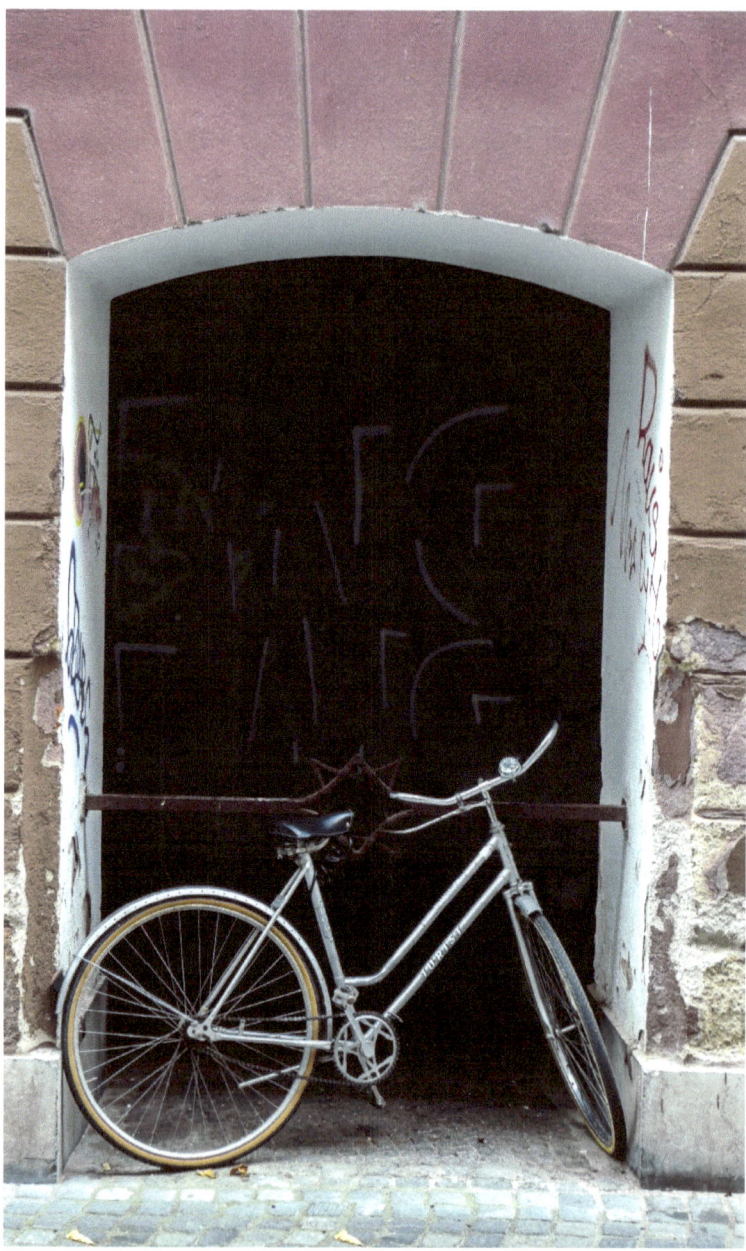

#Seen in Warsaw

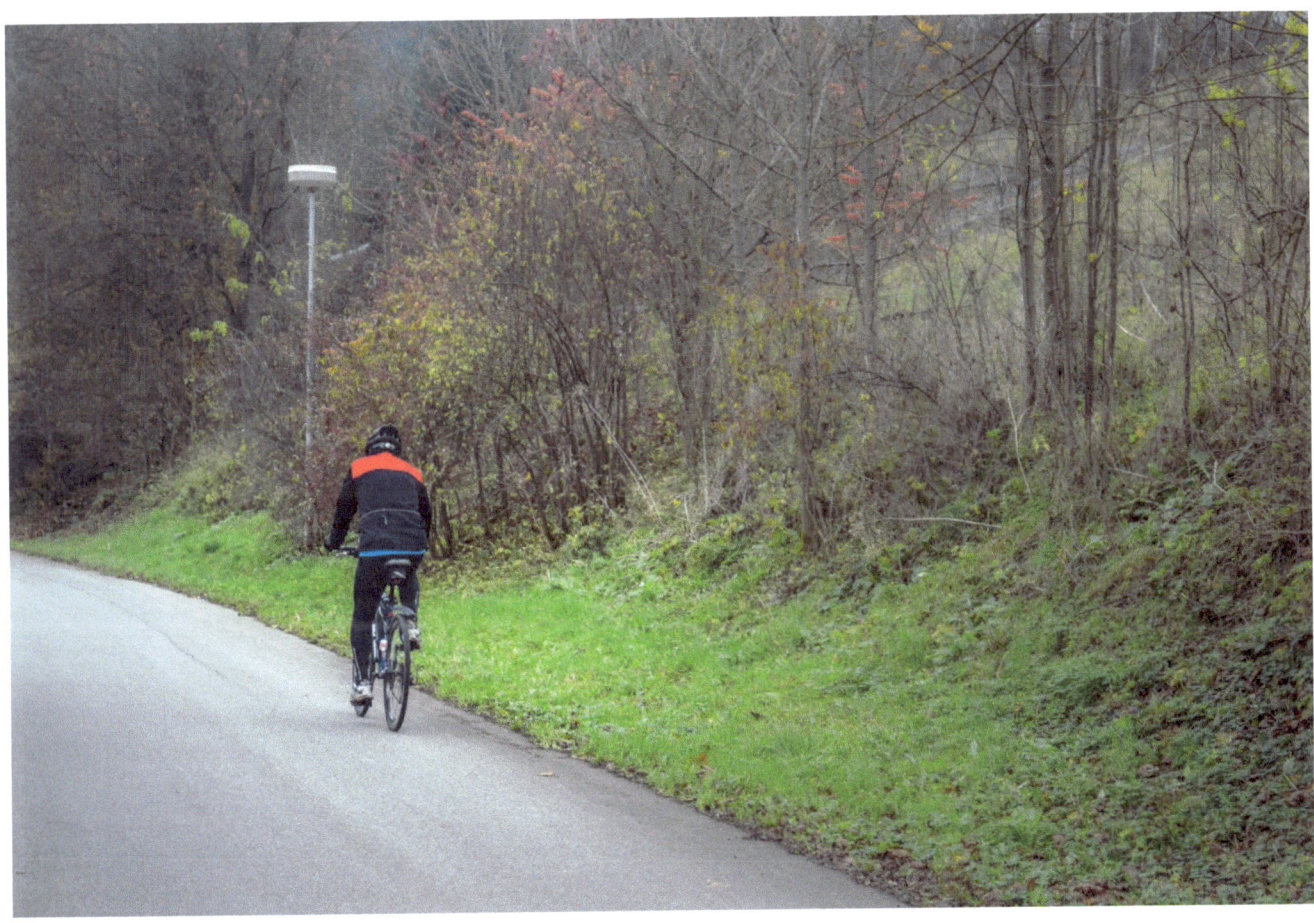

#Seen in Cesky Krumlov

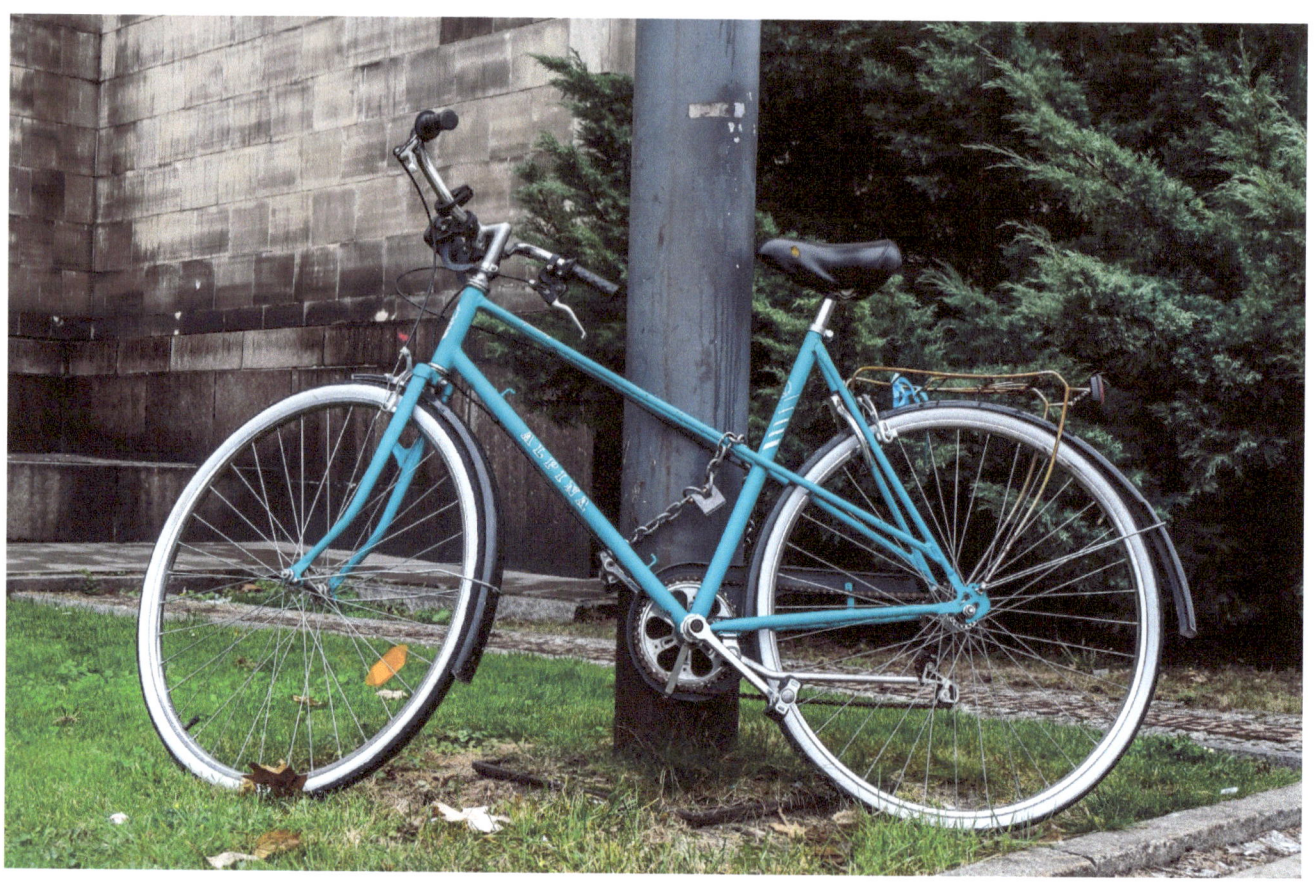

#Seen in Warsaw

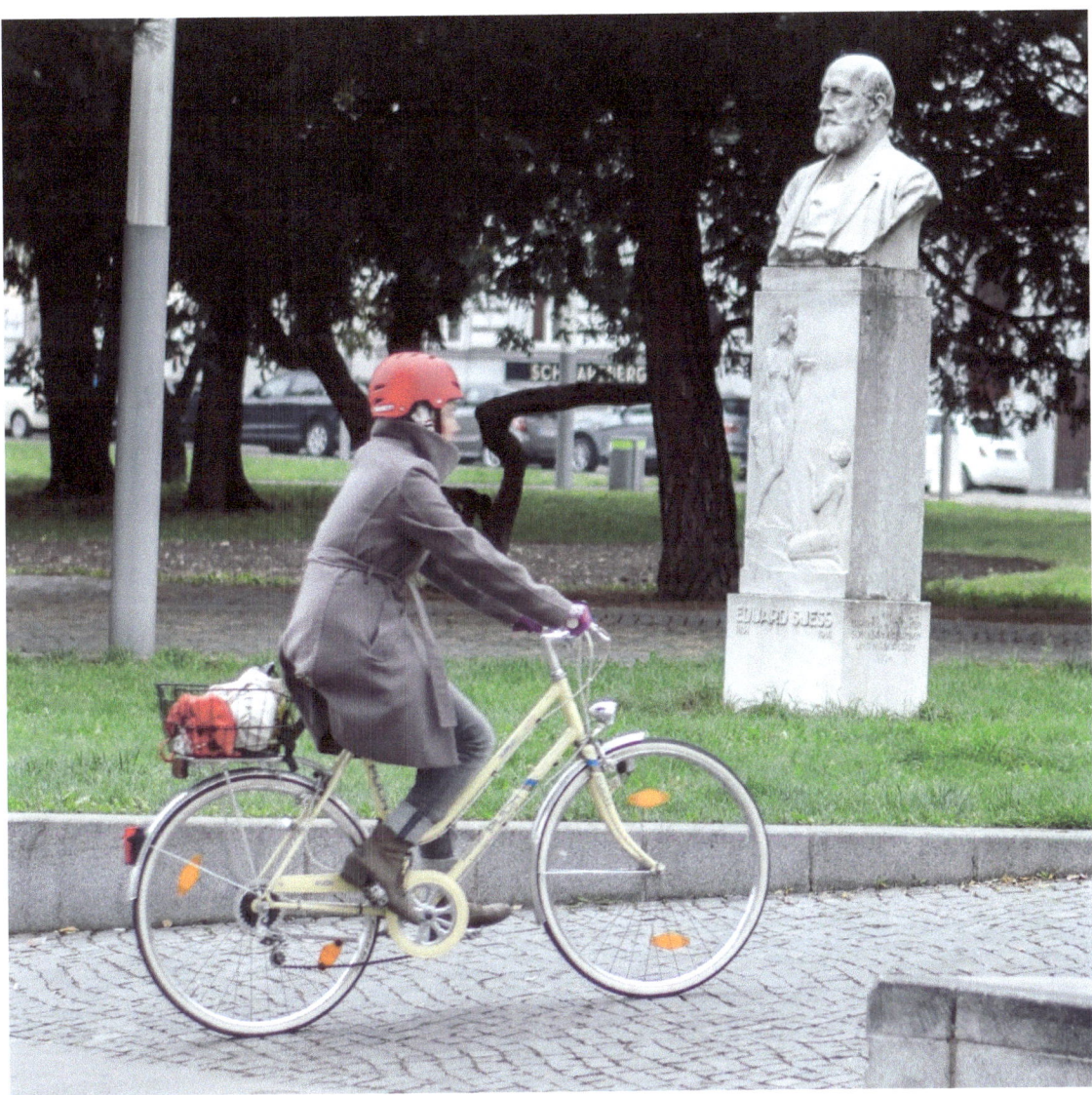

#Seen in Vienna

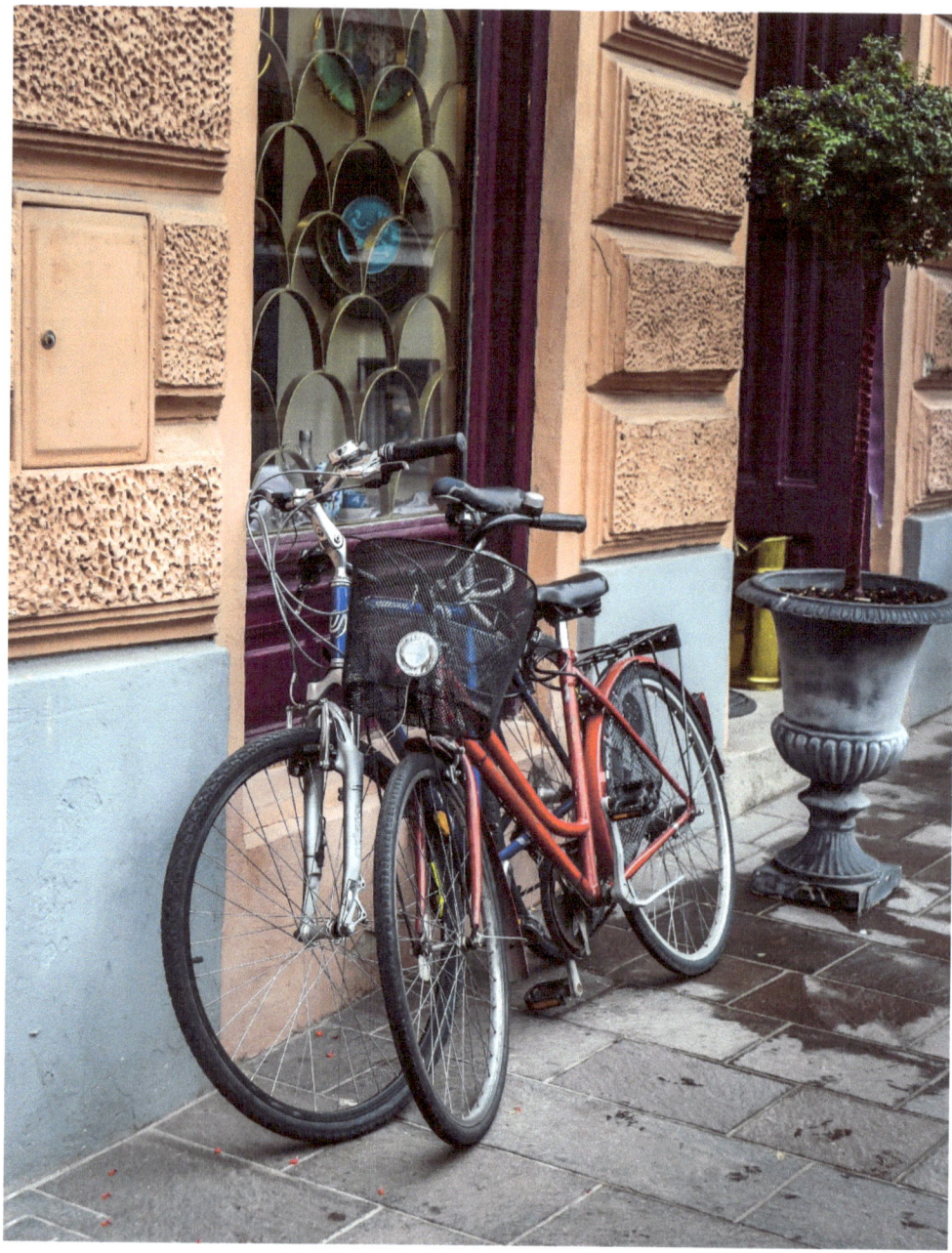

#Seen in Ljubljana

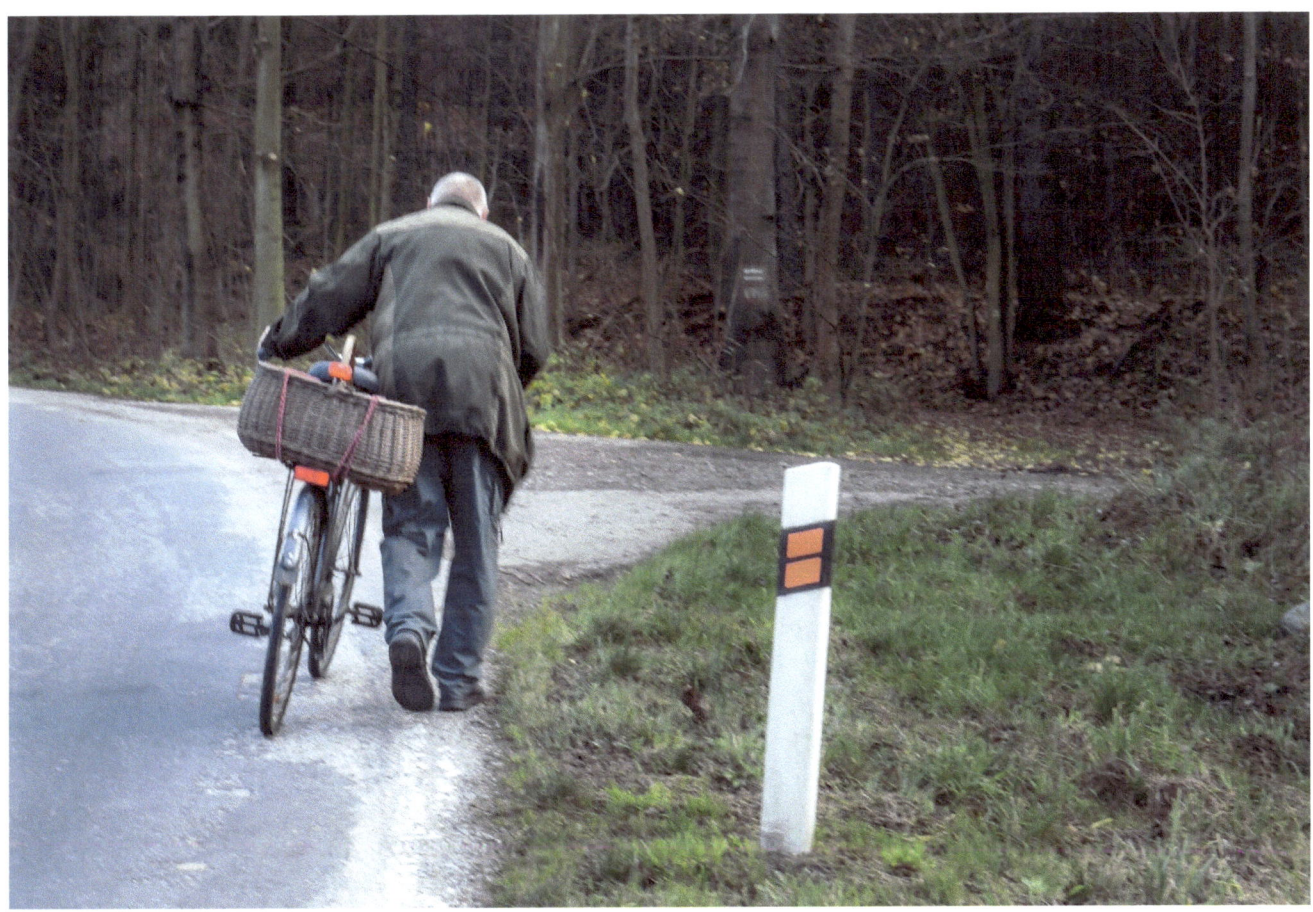

#Seen in Cesky Krumlov

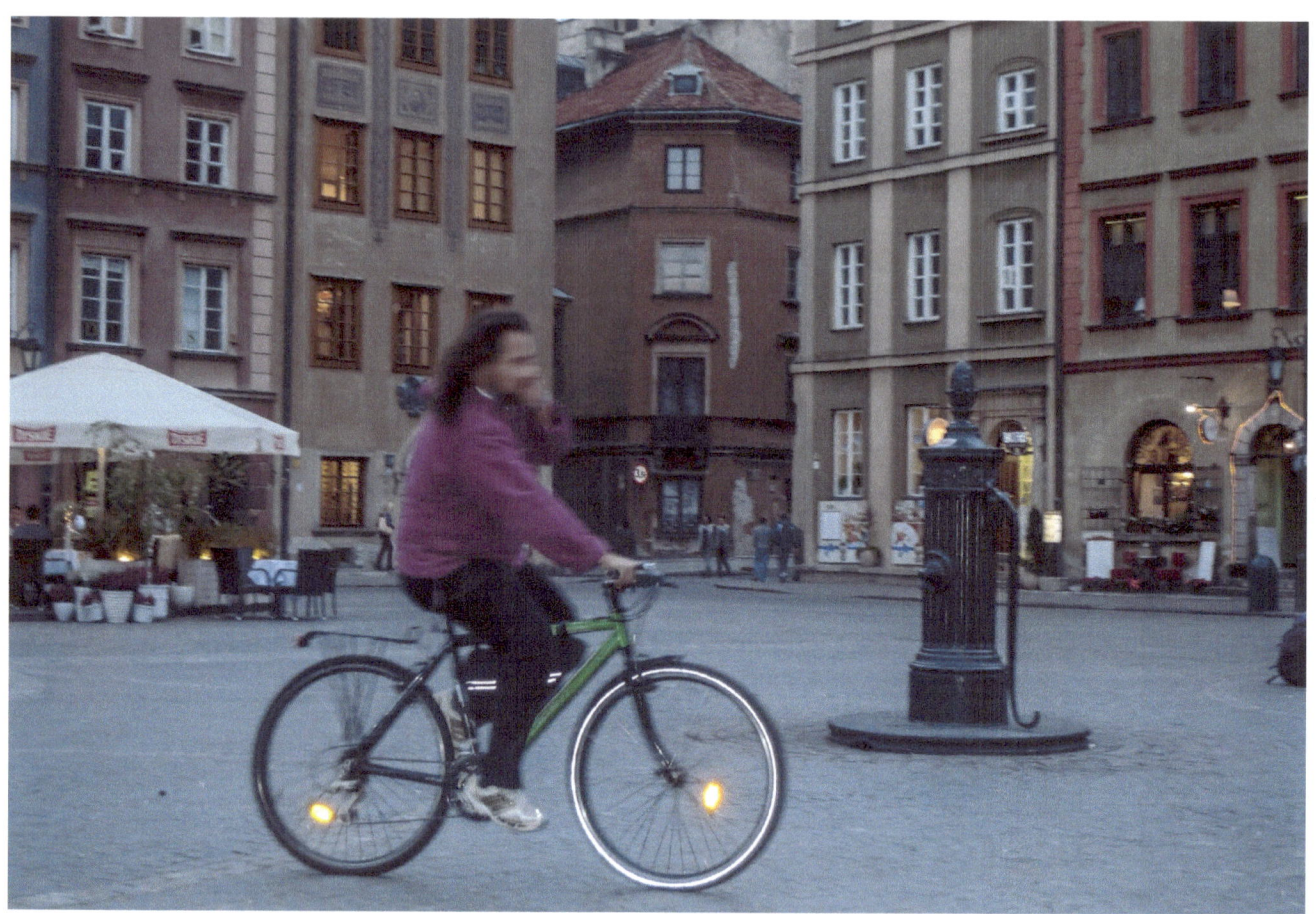

#Seen in Warsaw

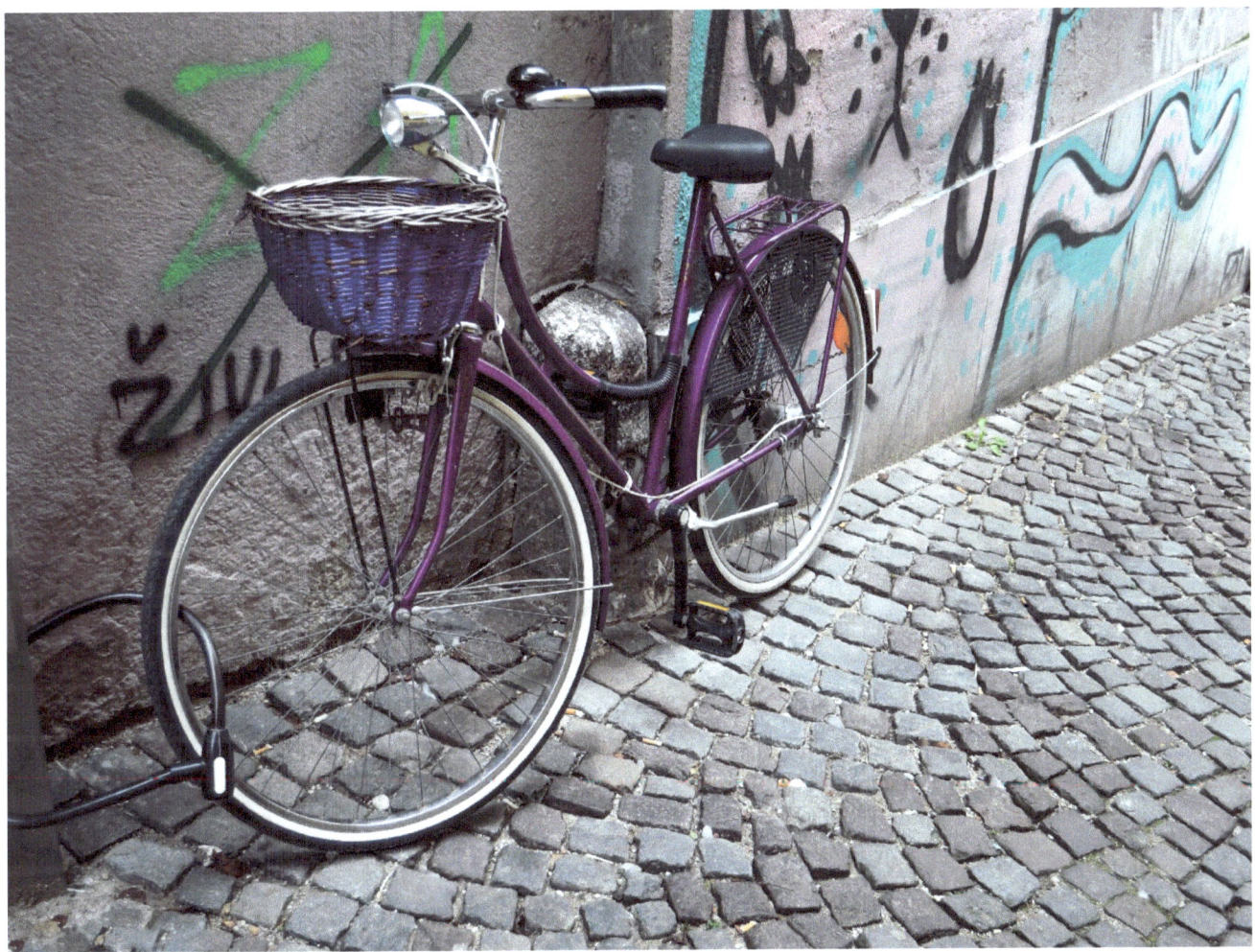

#Seen in Ljubljana

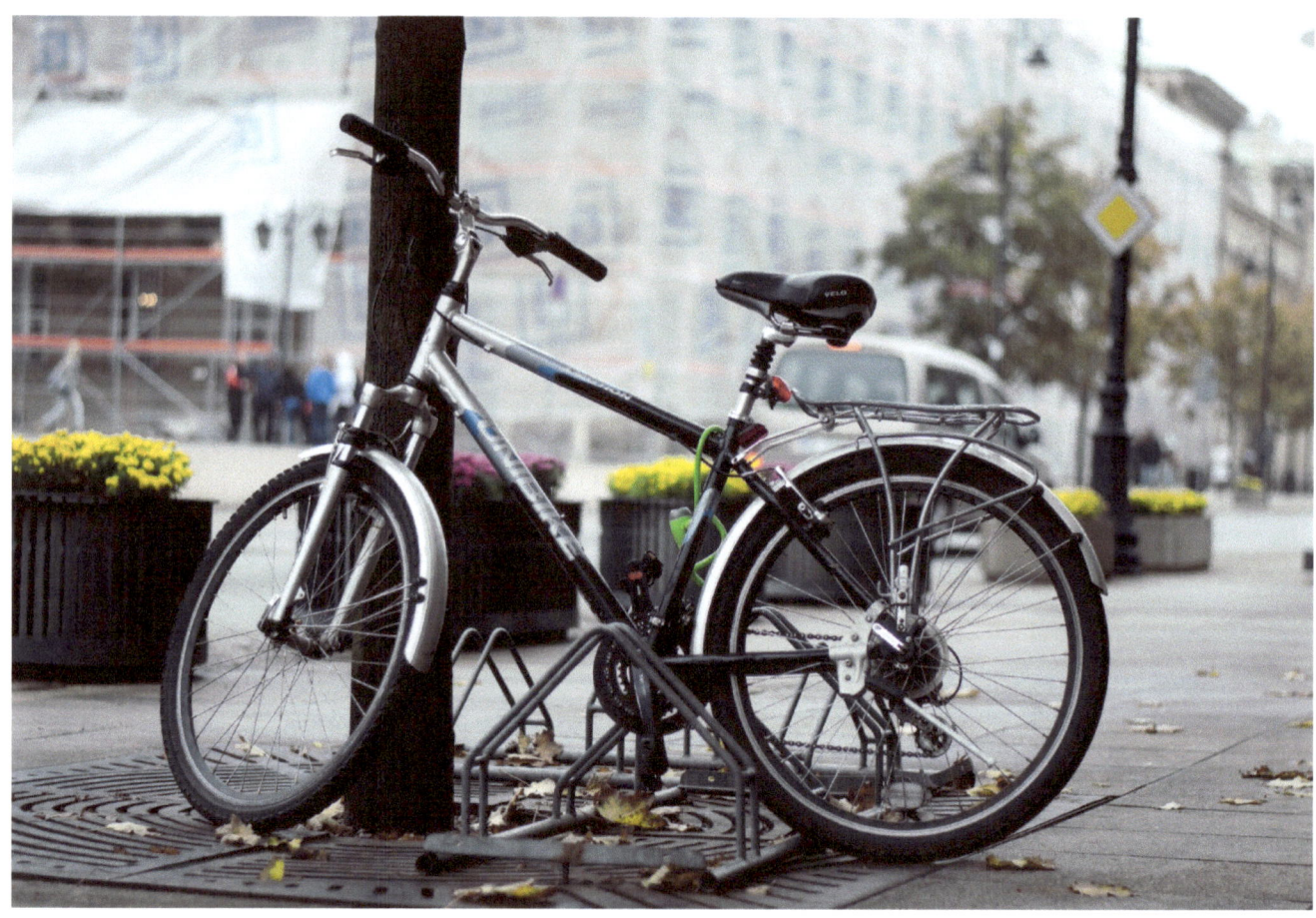

#Seen in Warsaw

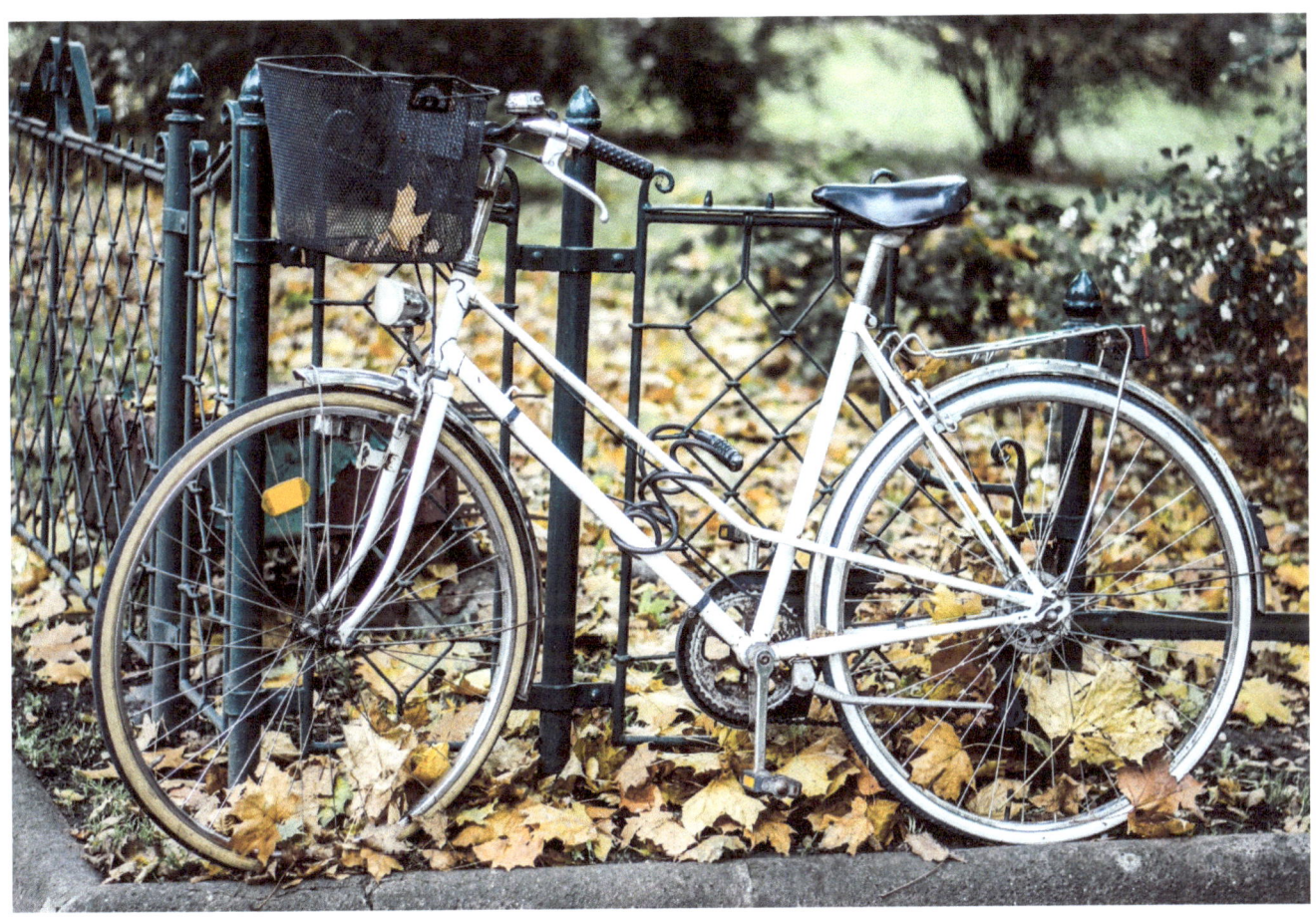

#Seen in Krakow

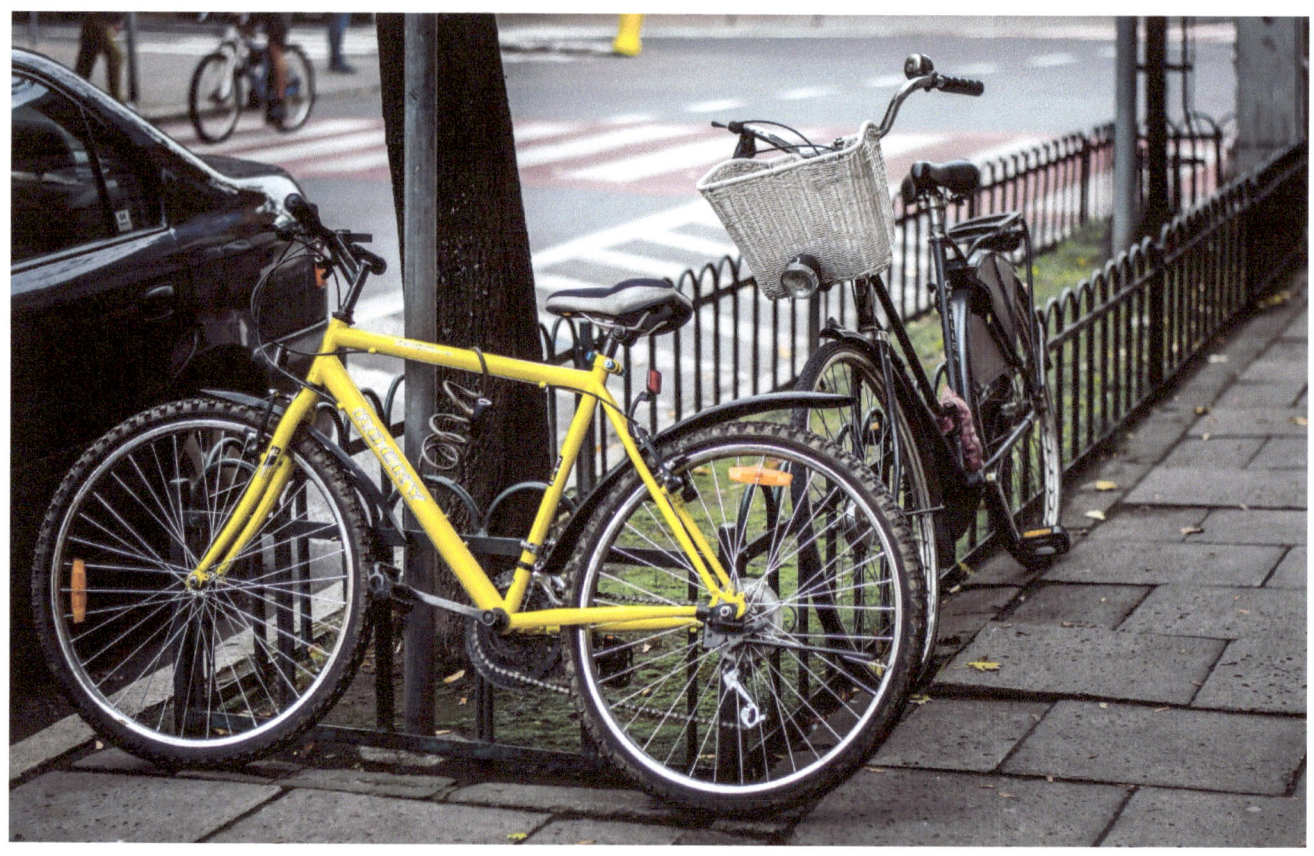

#Seen in Warsaw

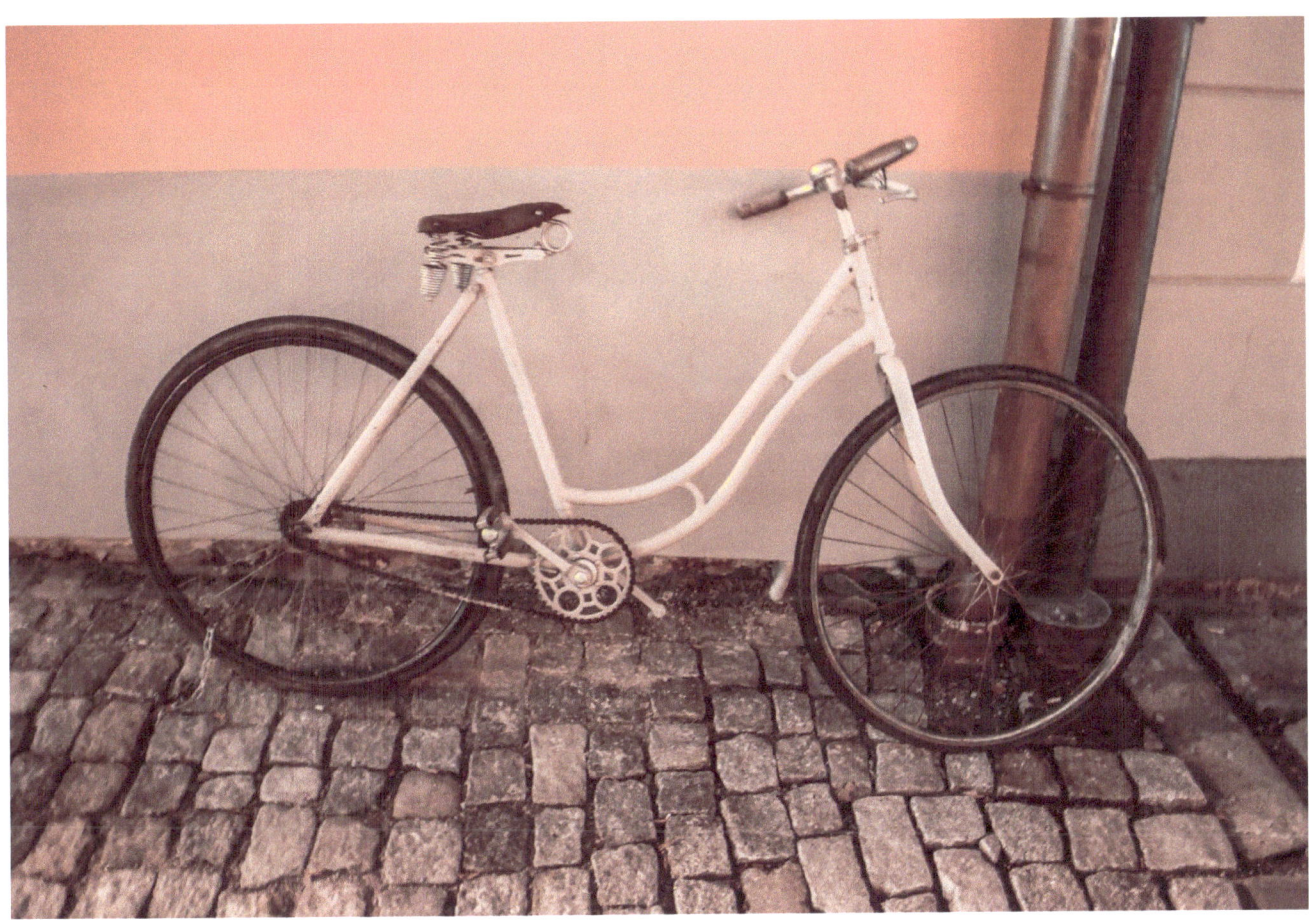

#Seen in Cesky Krumlov

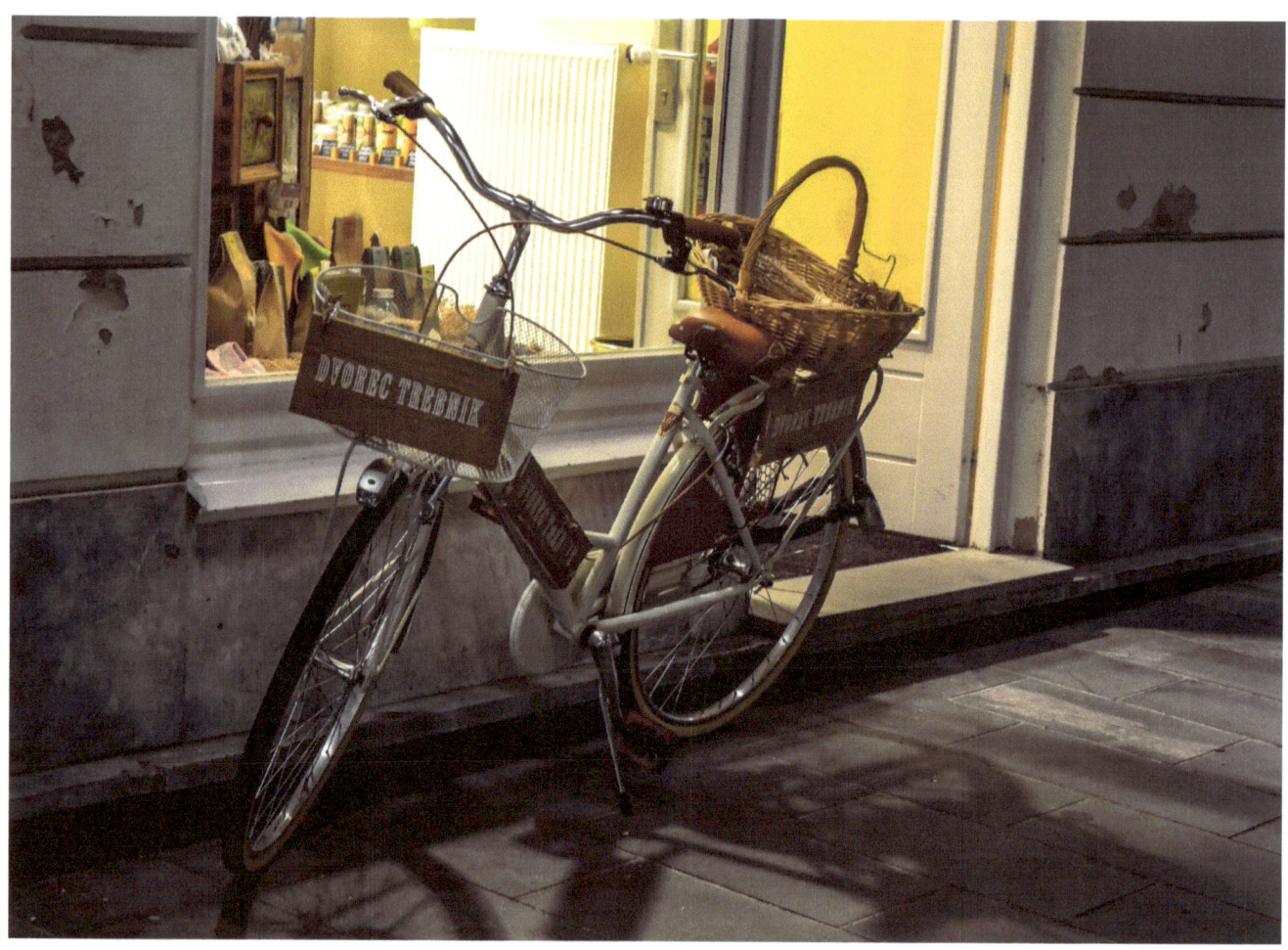

#Seen in Ljubljana

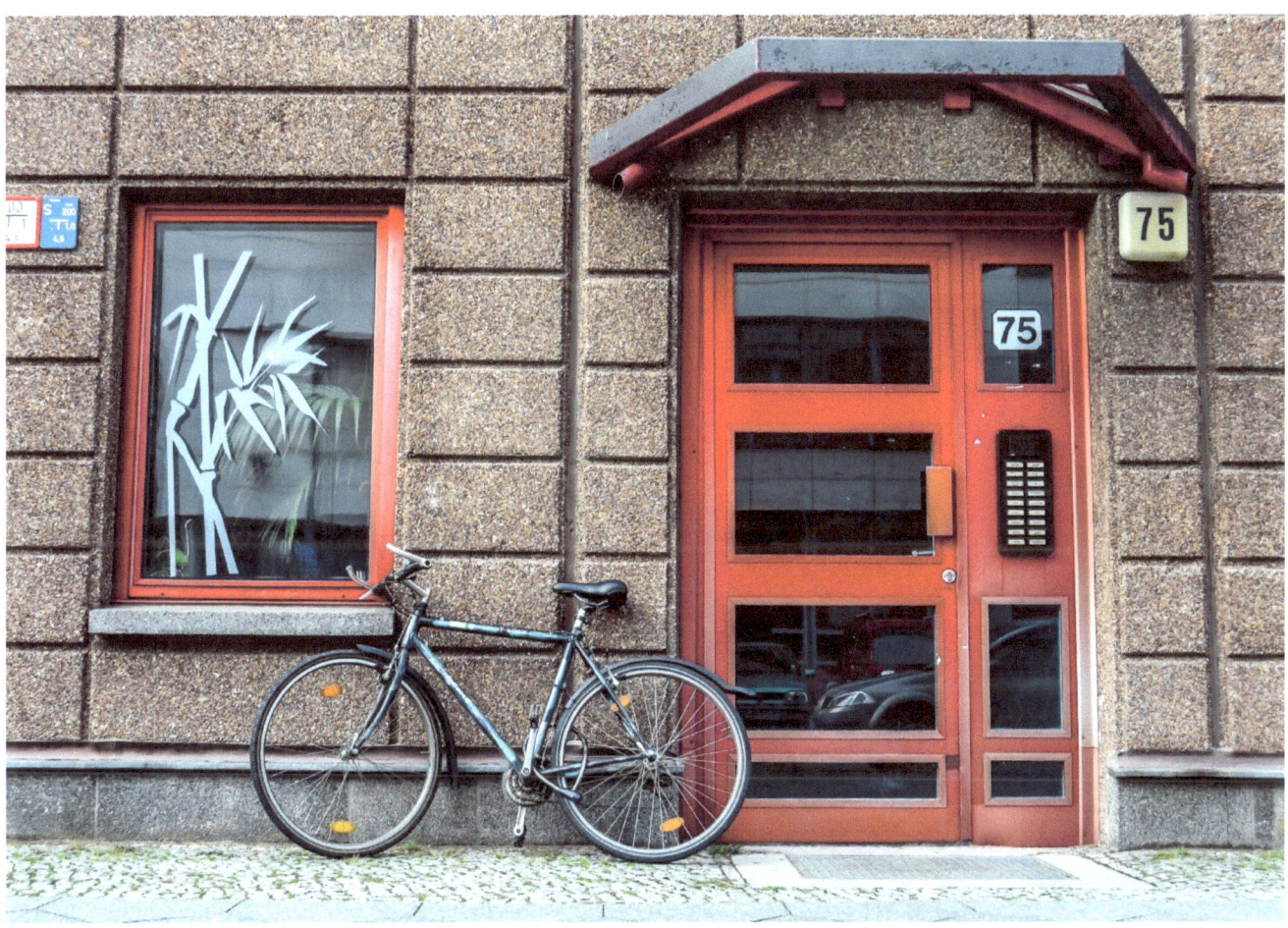

#Seen in Berlin

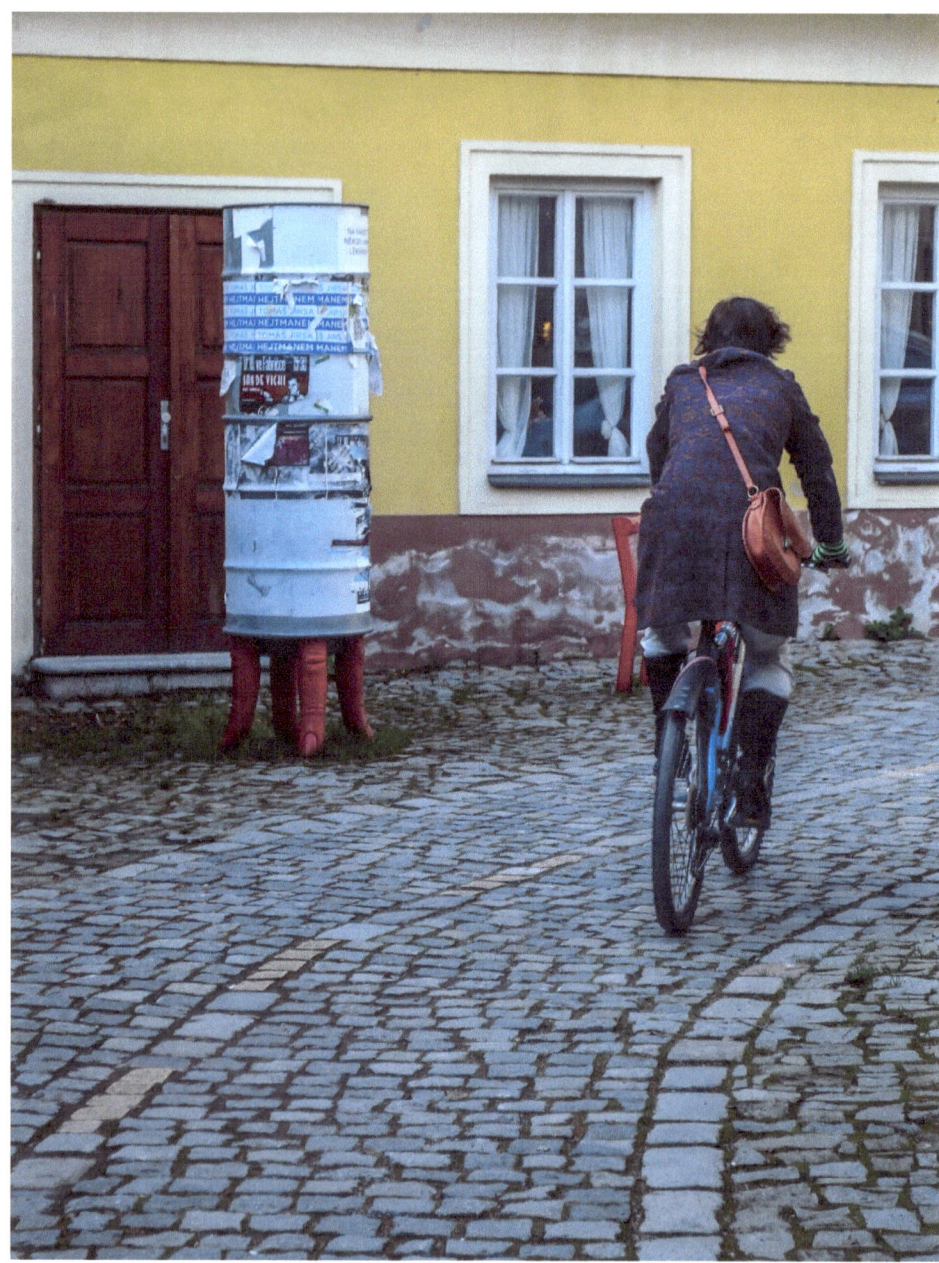

#Seen in Cesky Krumlov

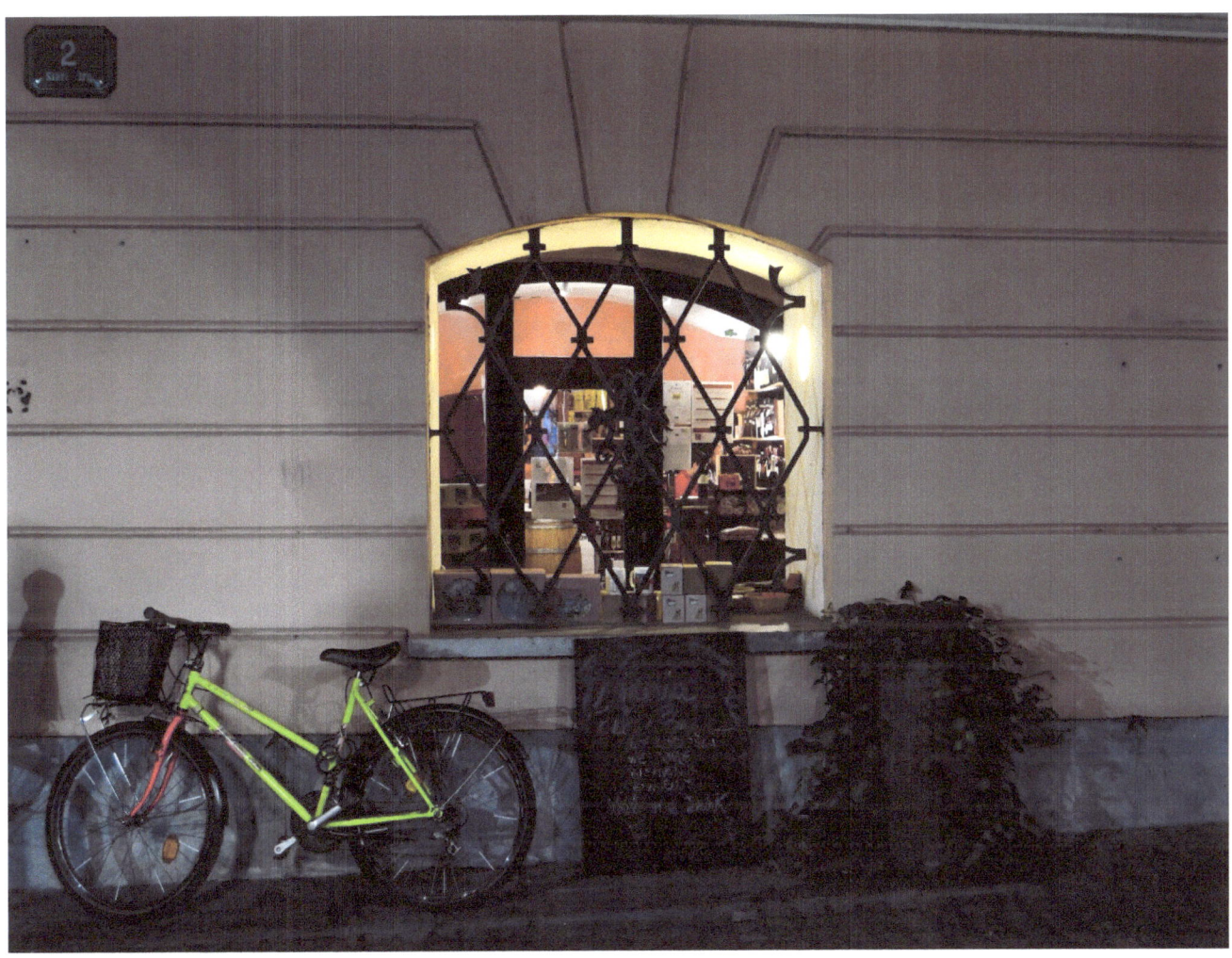

#Seen in Ljubljana

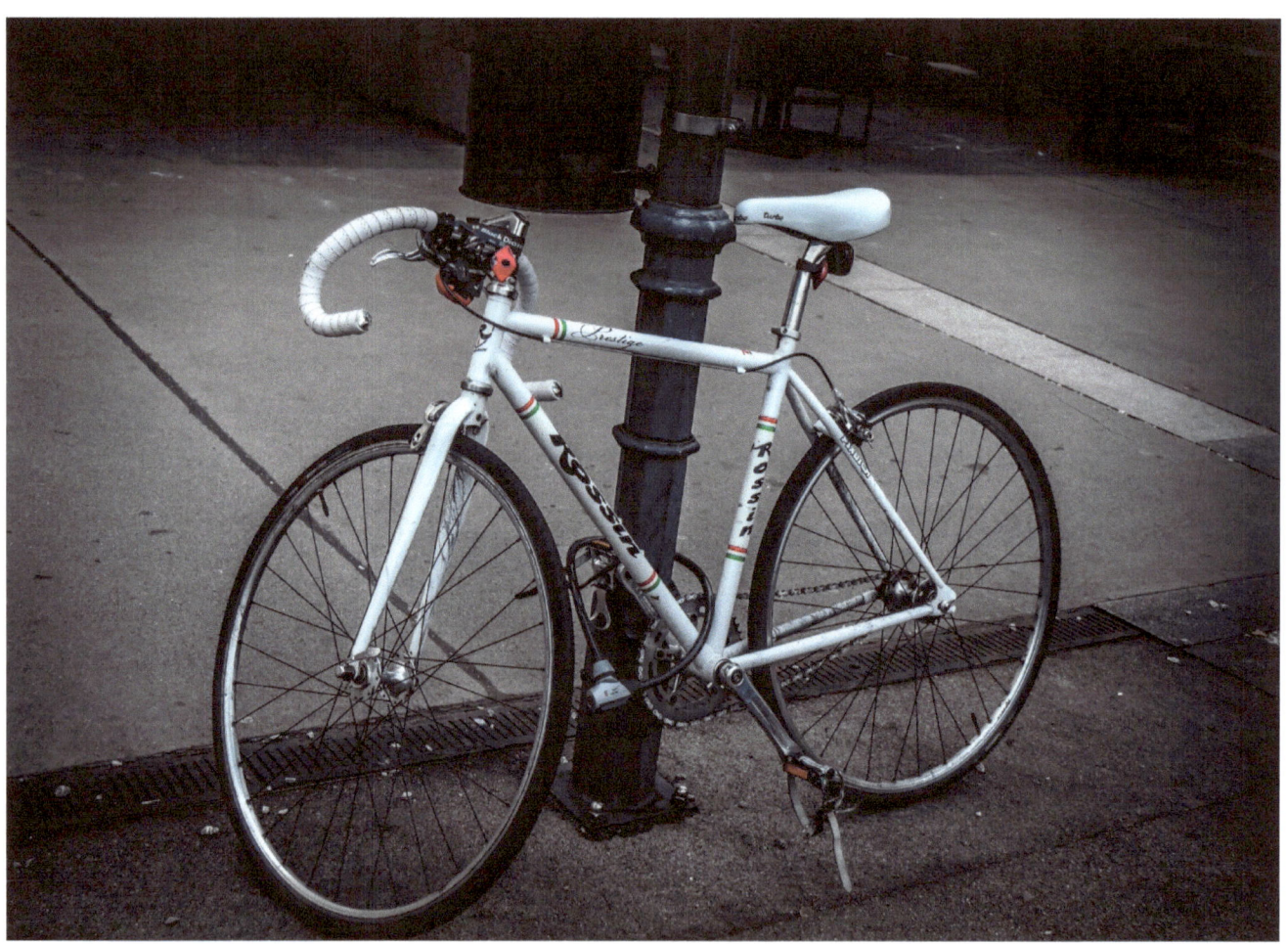

#Seen in Vienna

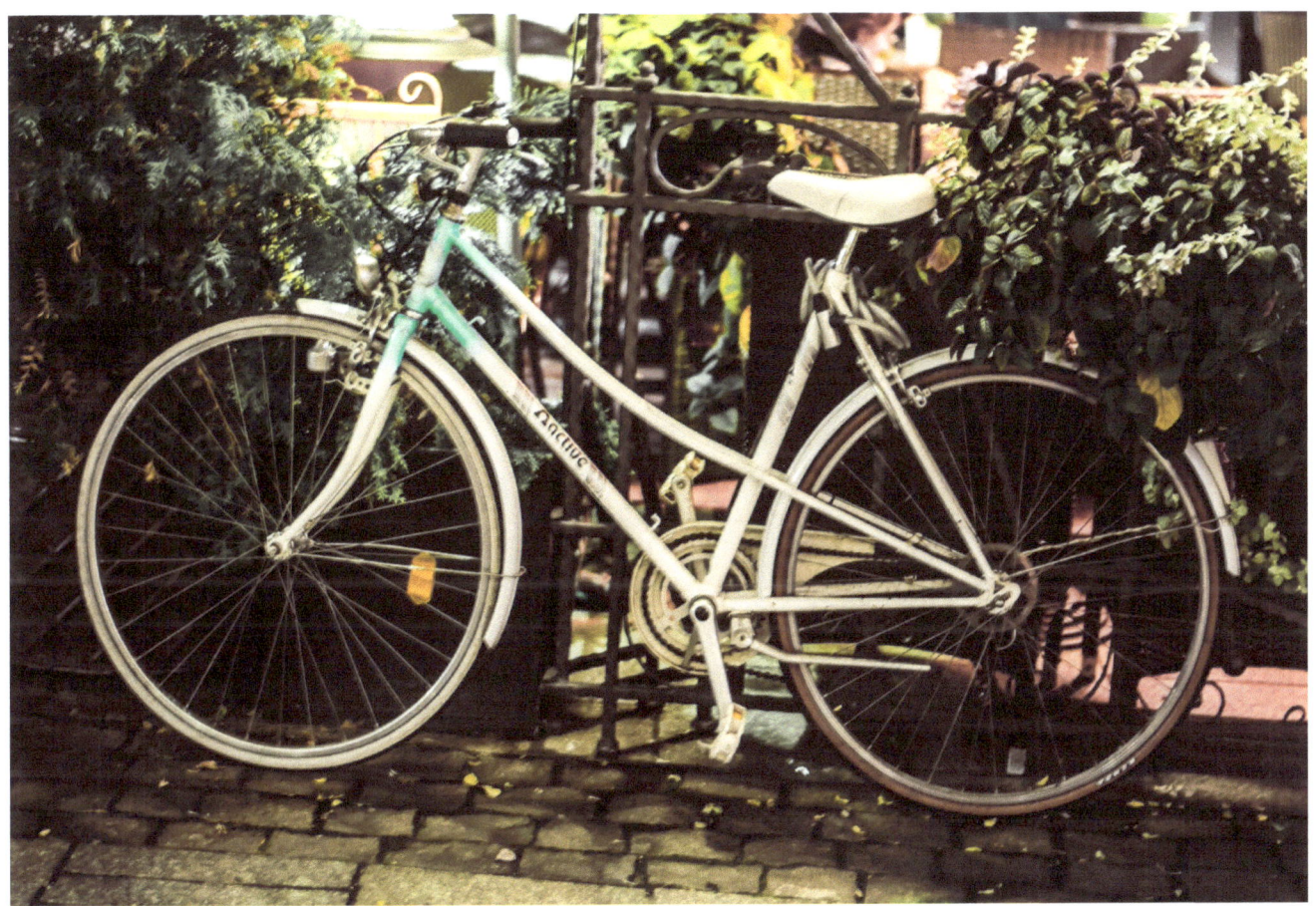

#Seen in Krakow

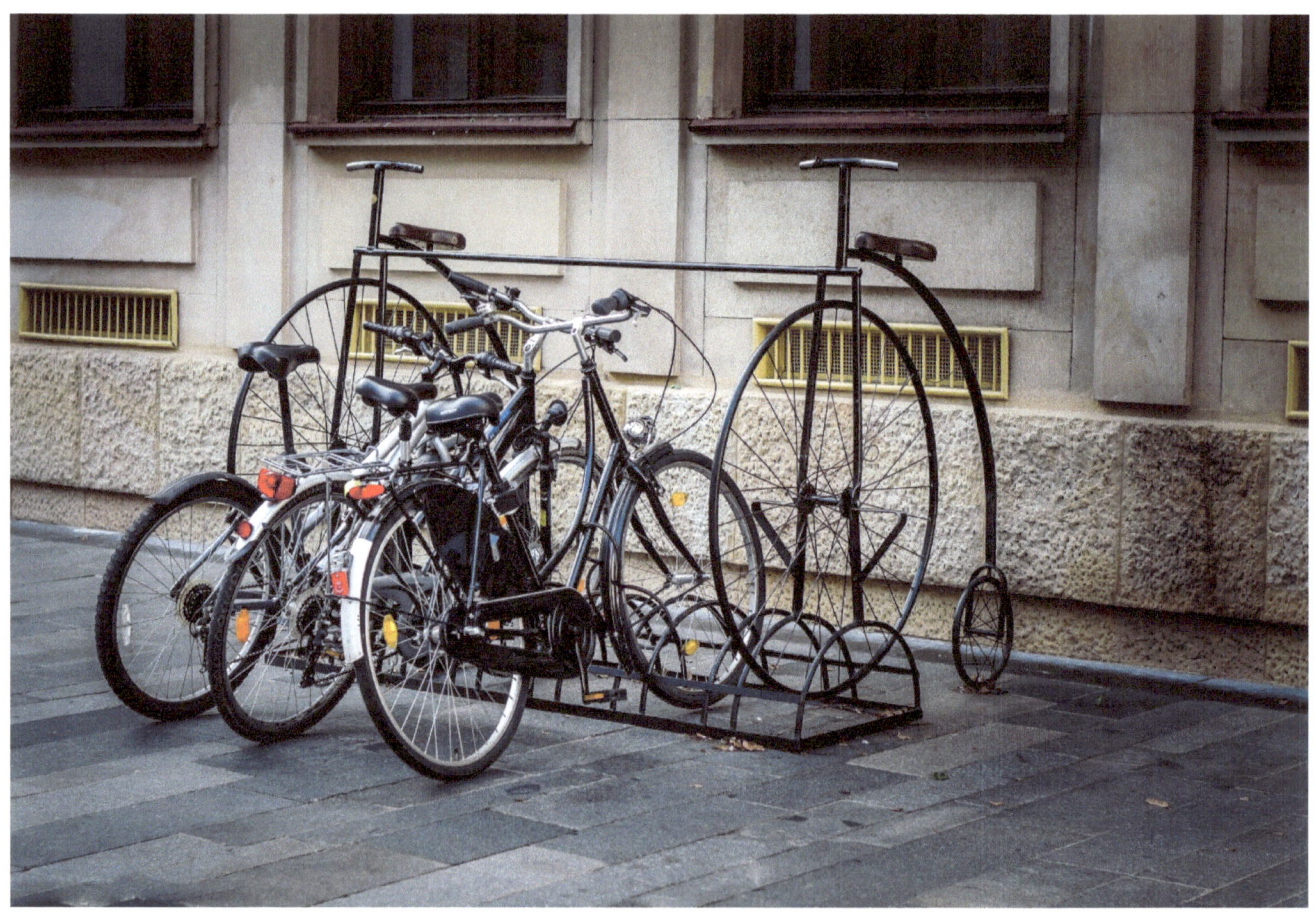

#Seen in Bratislava

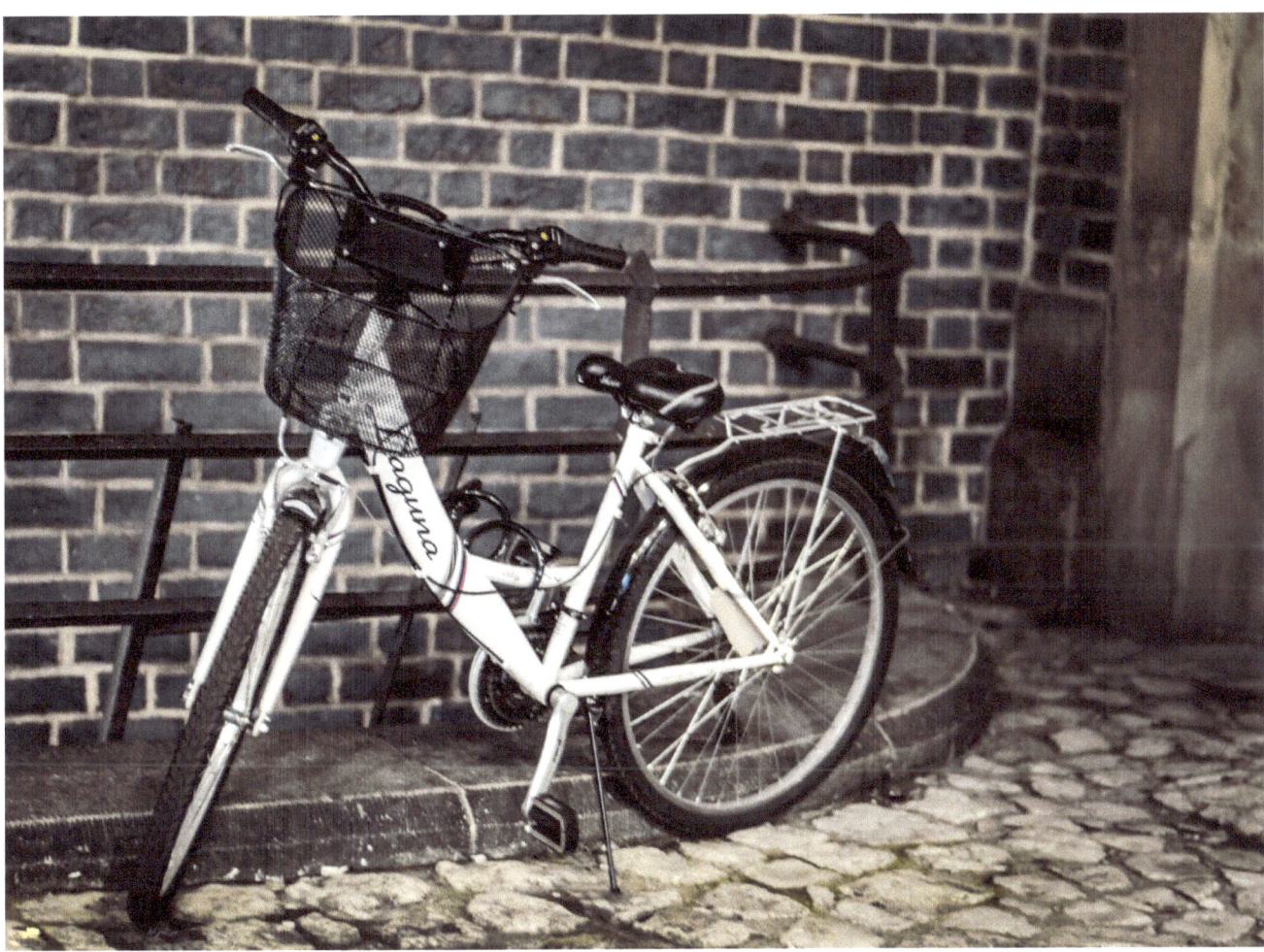

#Seen in Krakow

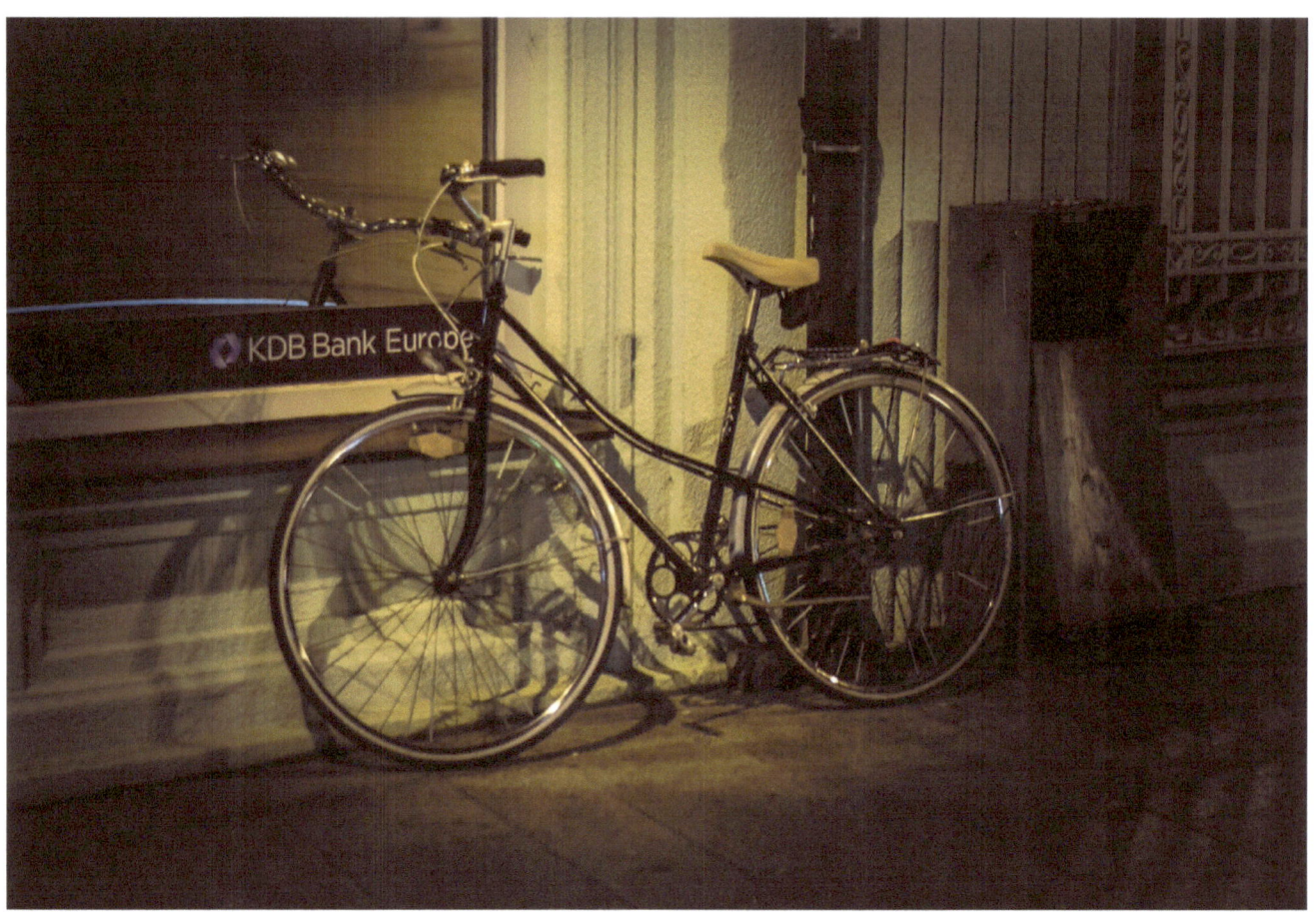

#Seen in Bratislava

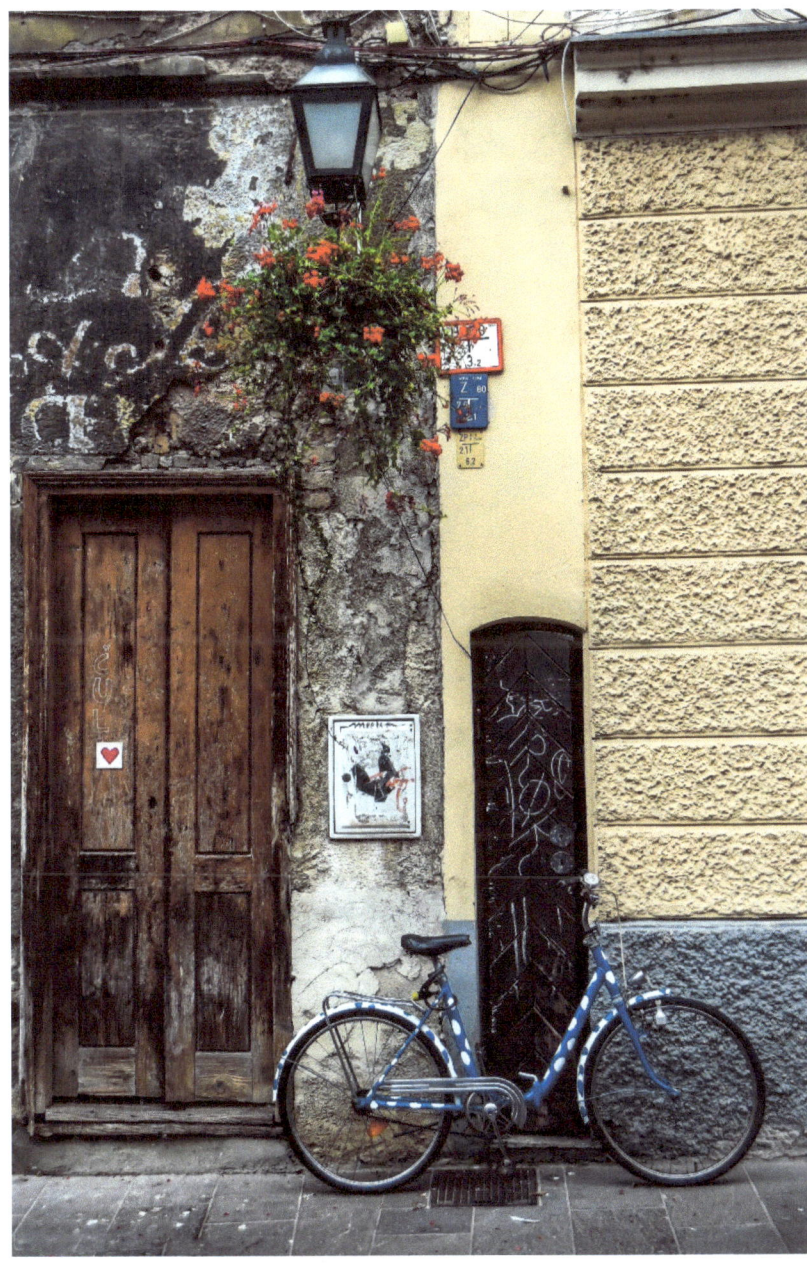

#Seen in Ljubljana

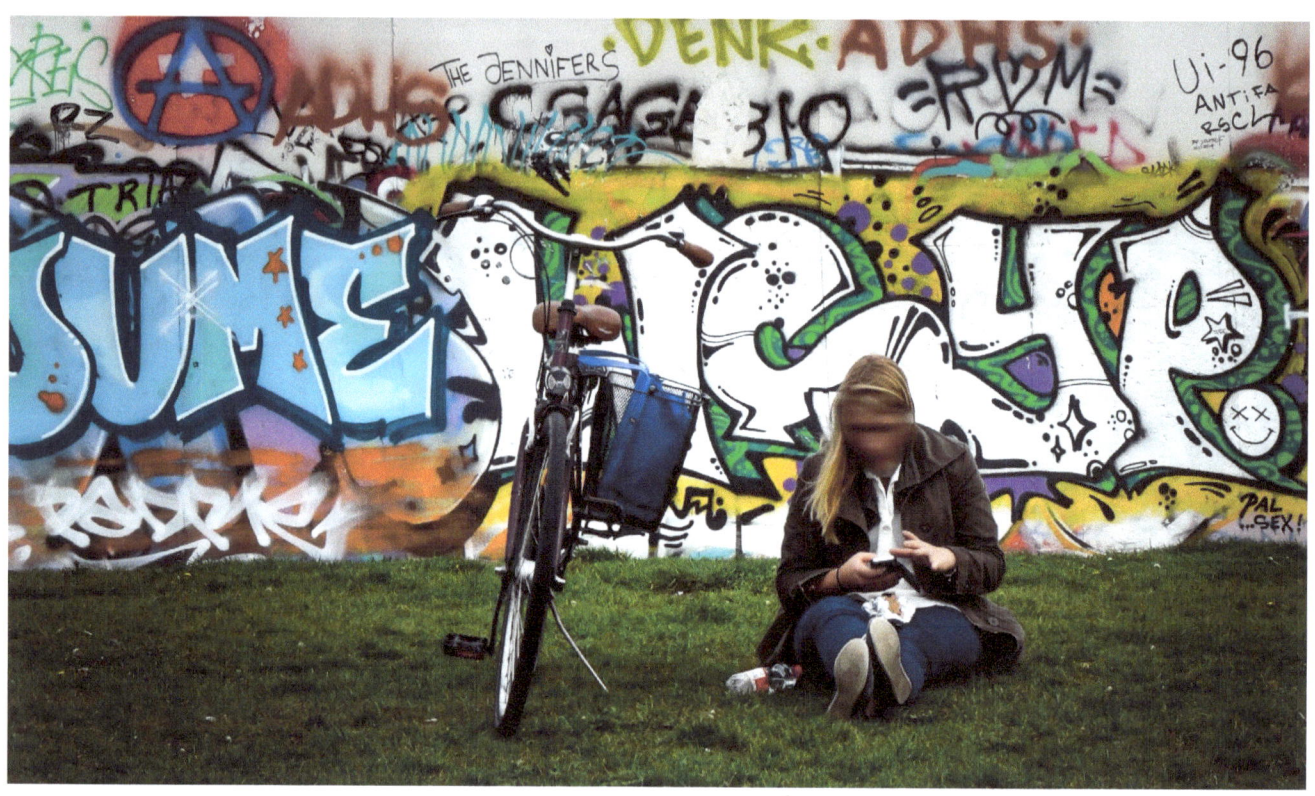

#Seen in Berlin

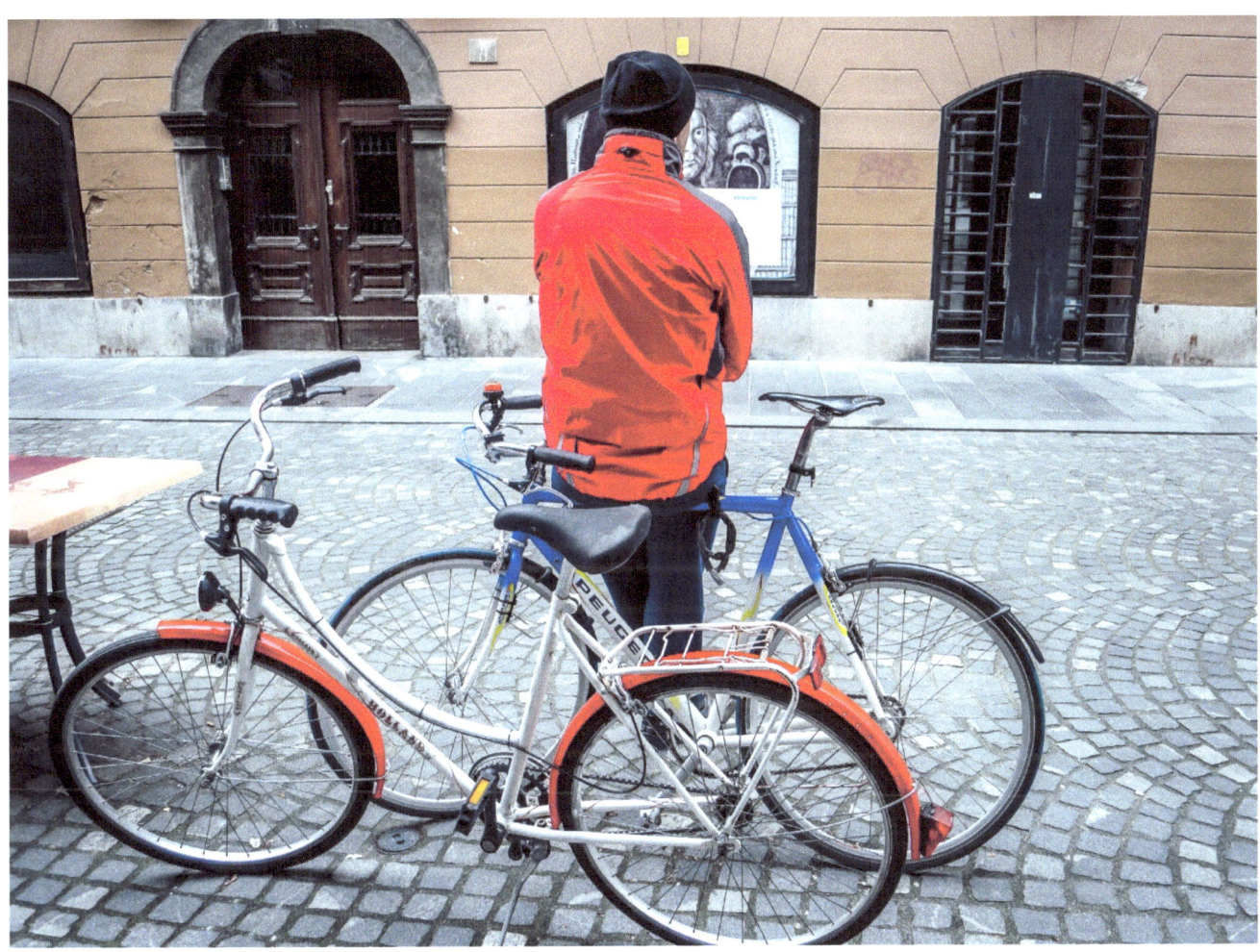

#Seen in Ljubljana

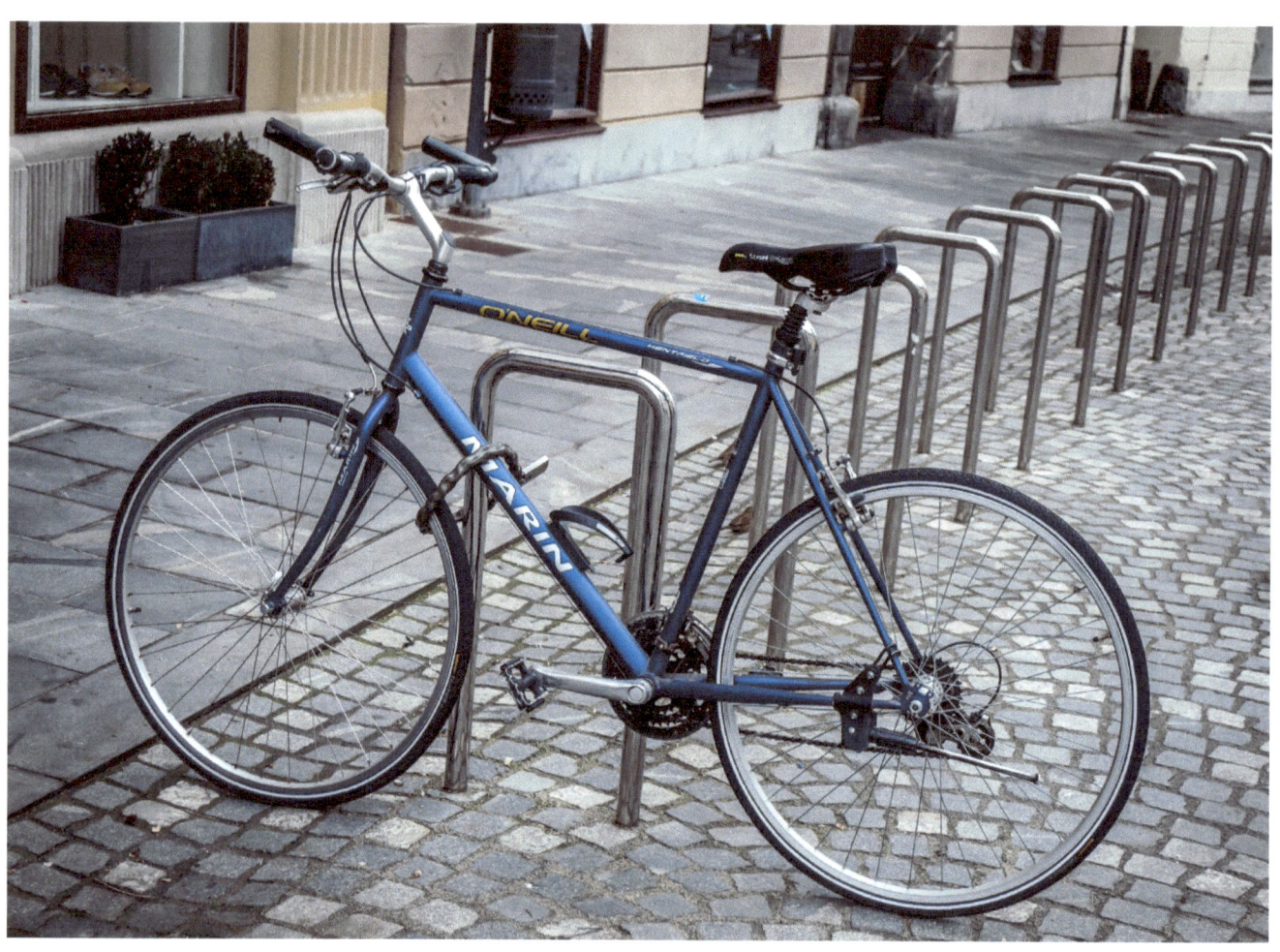

#Seen in Ljubljana

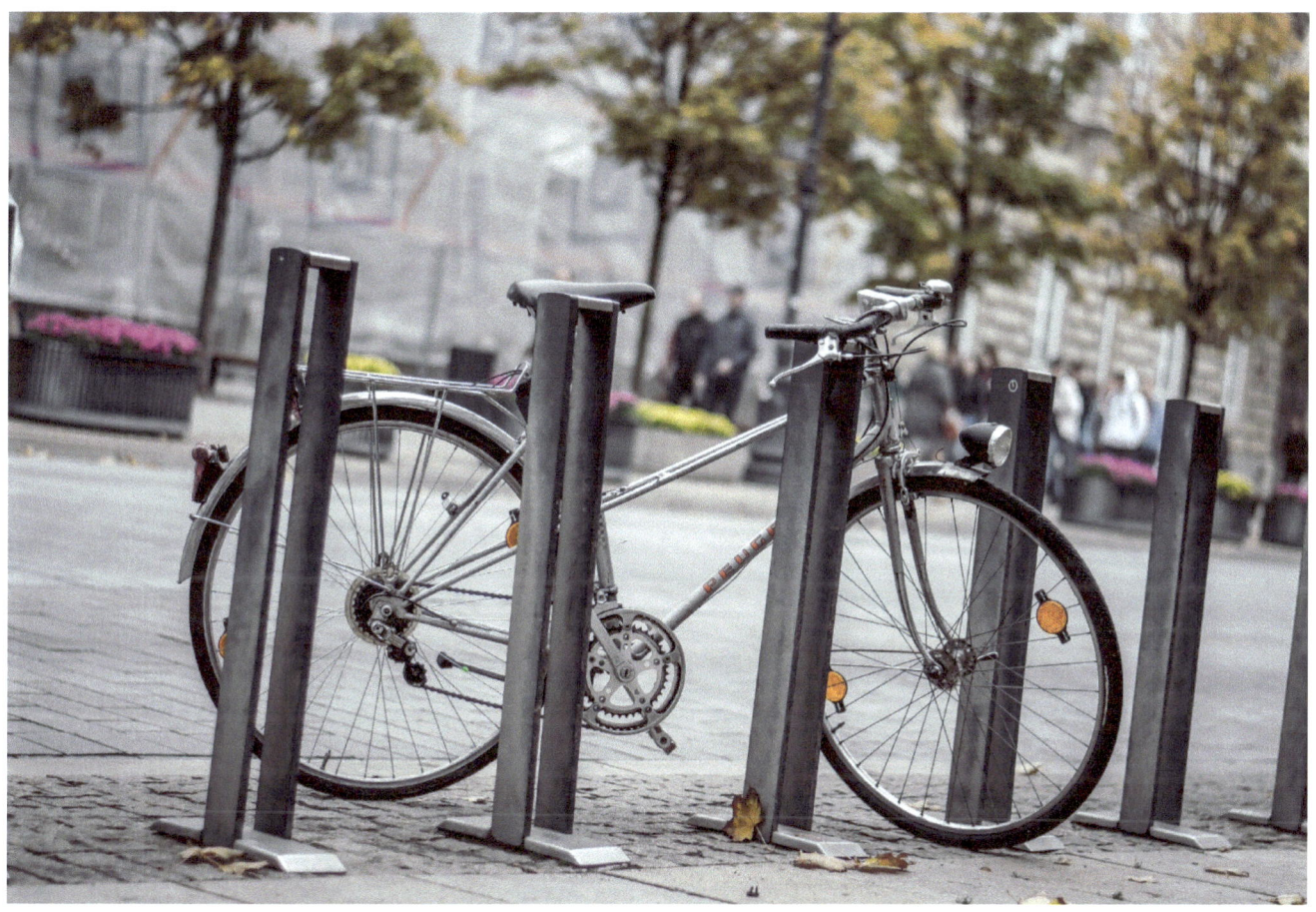

#Seen in Warsaw

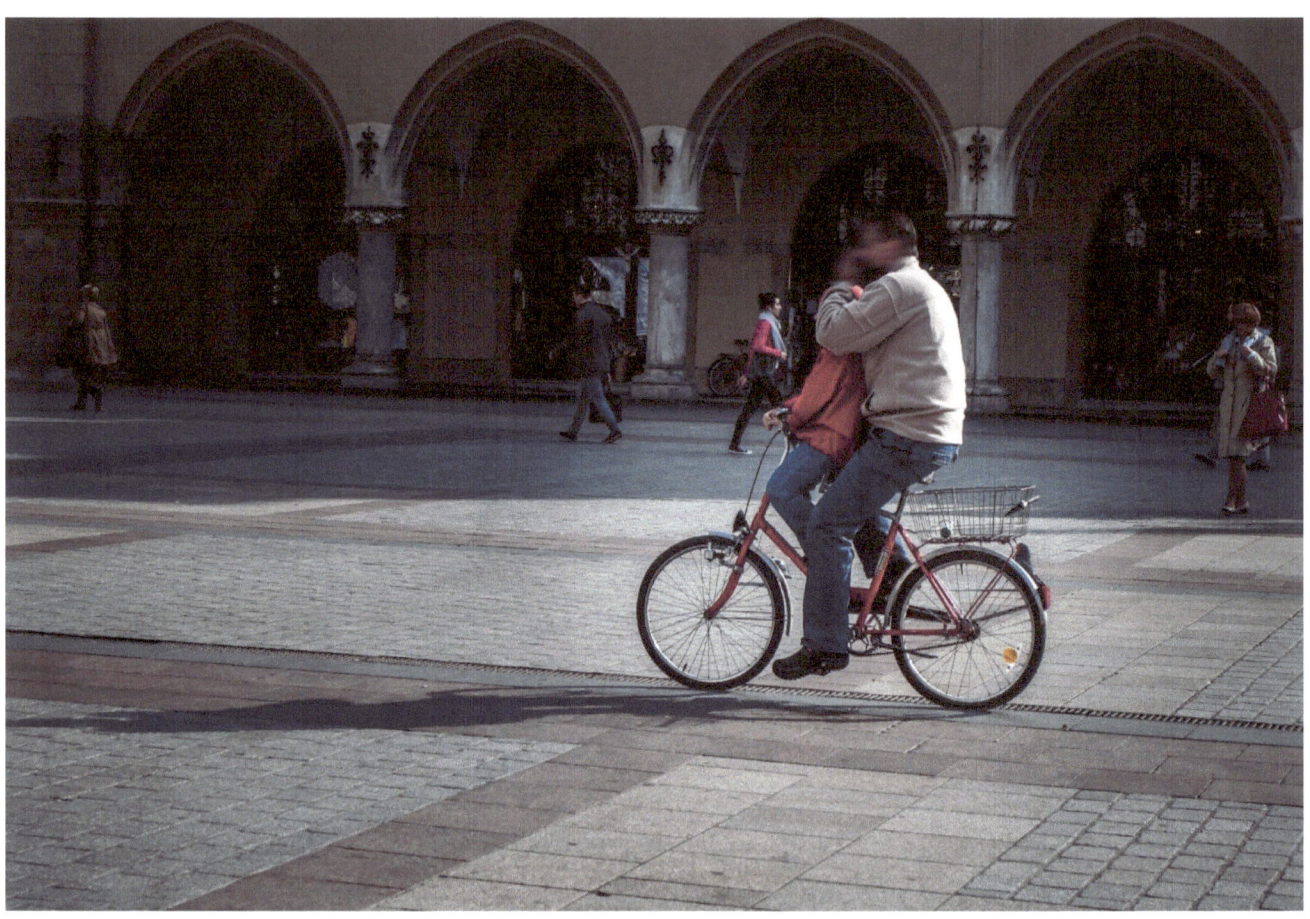

#Seen in Krakow

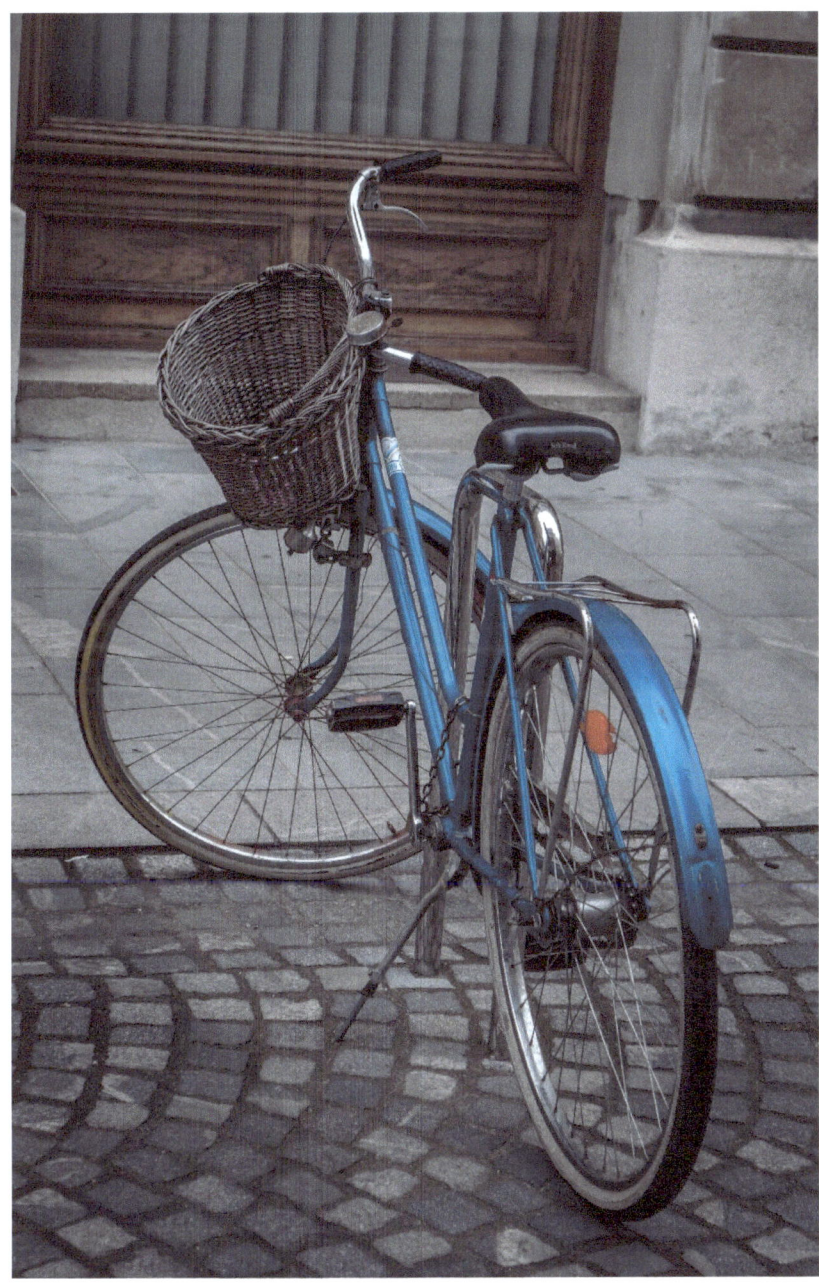

#Seen in Ljubljana

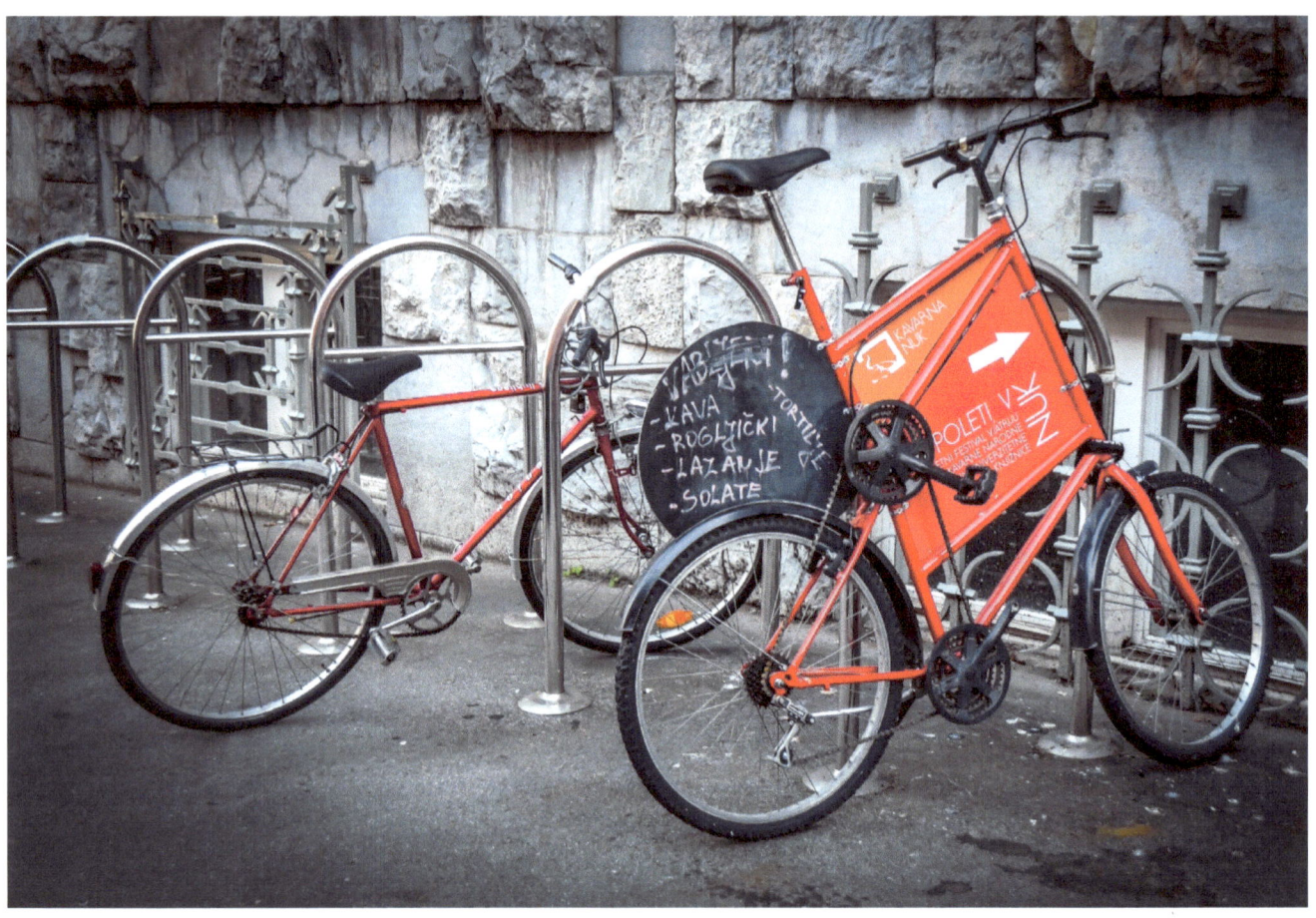

#Seen in Ljubljana

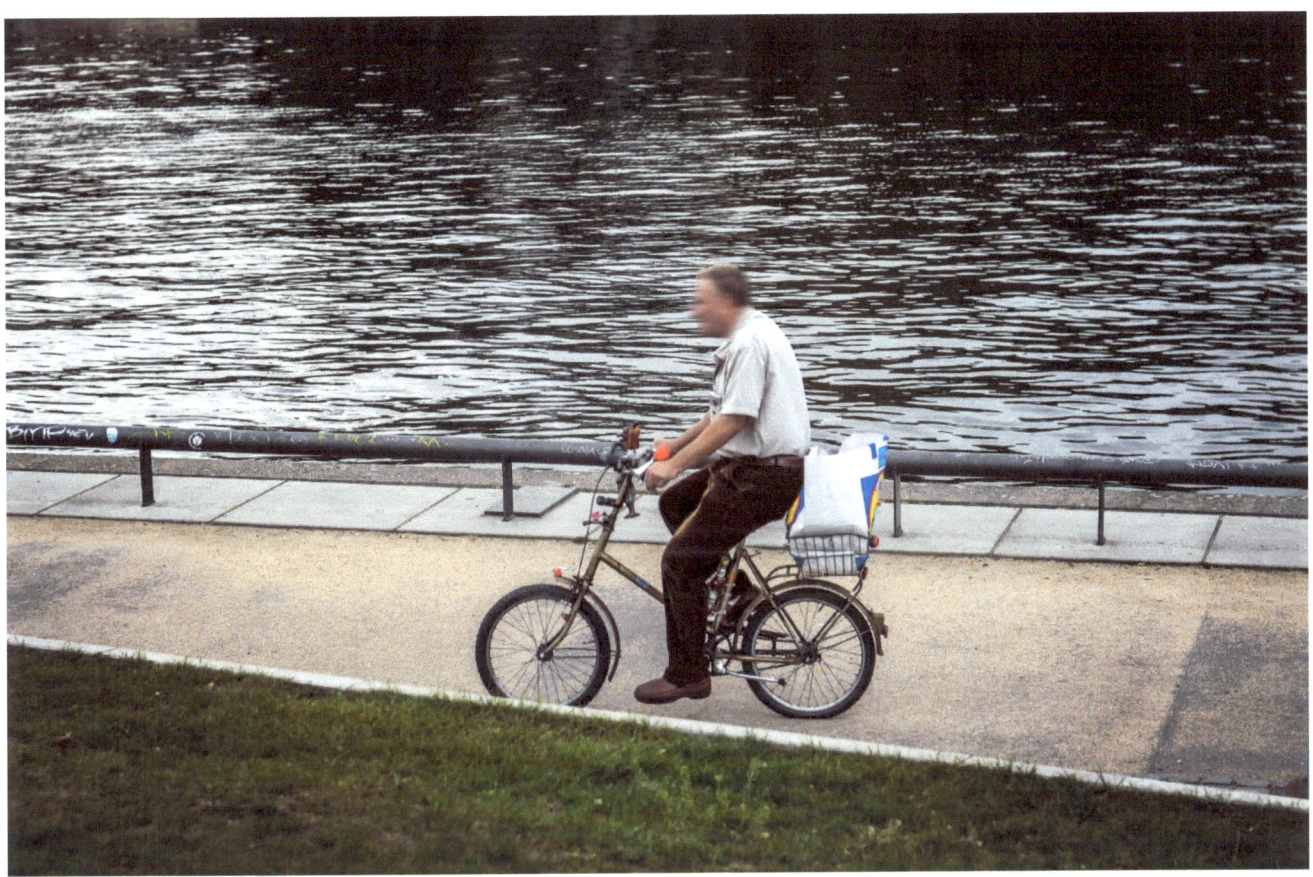

#Seen in Berlin

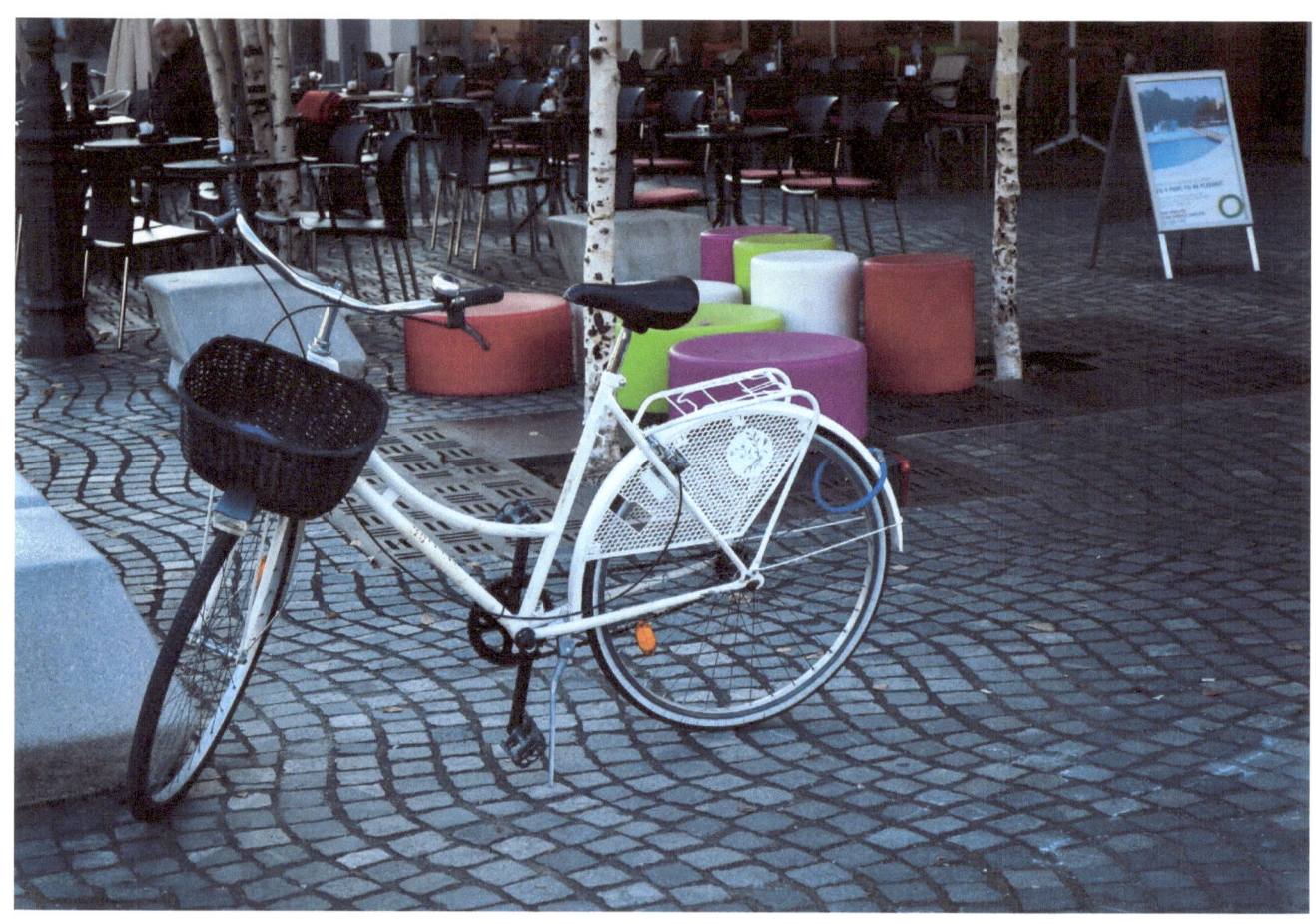

#Seen in Ljubljana

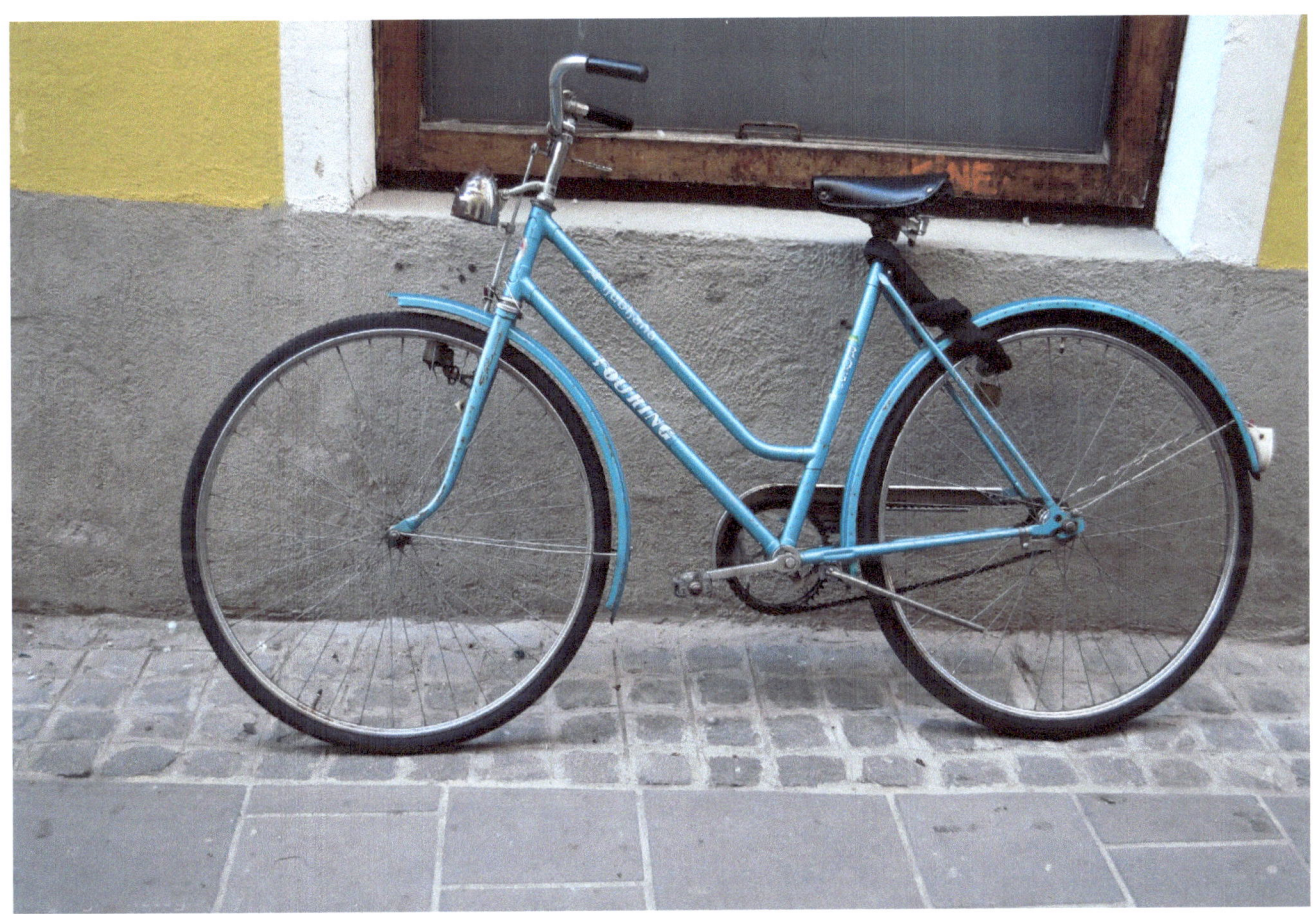

#Seen in Ljubljana

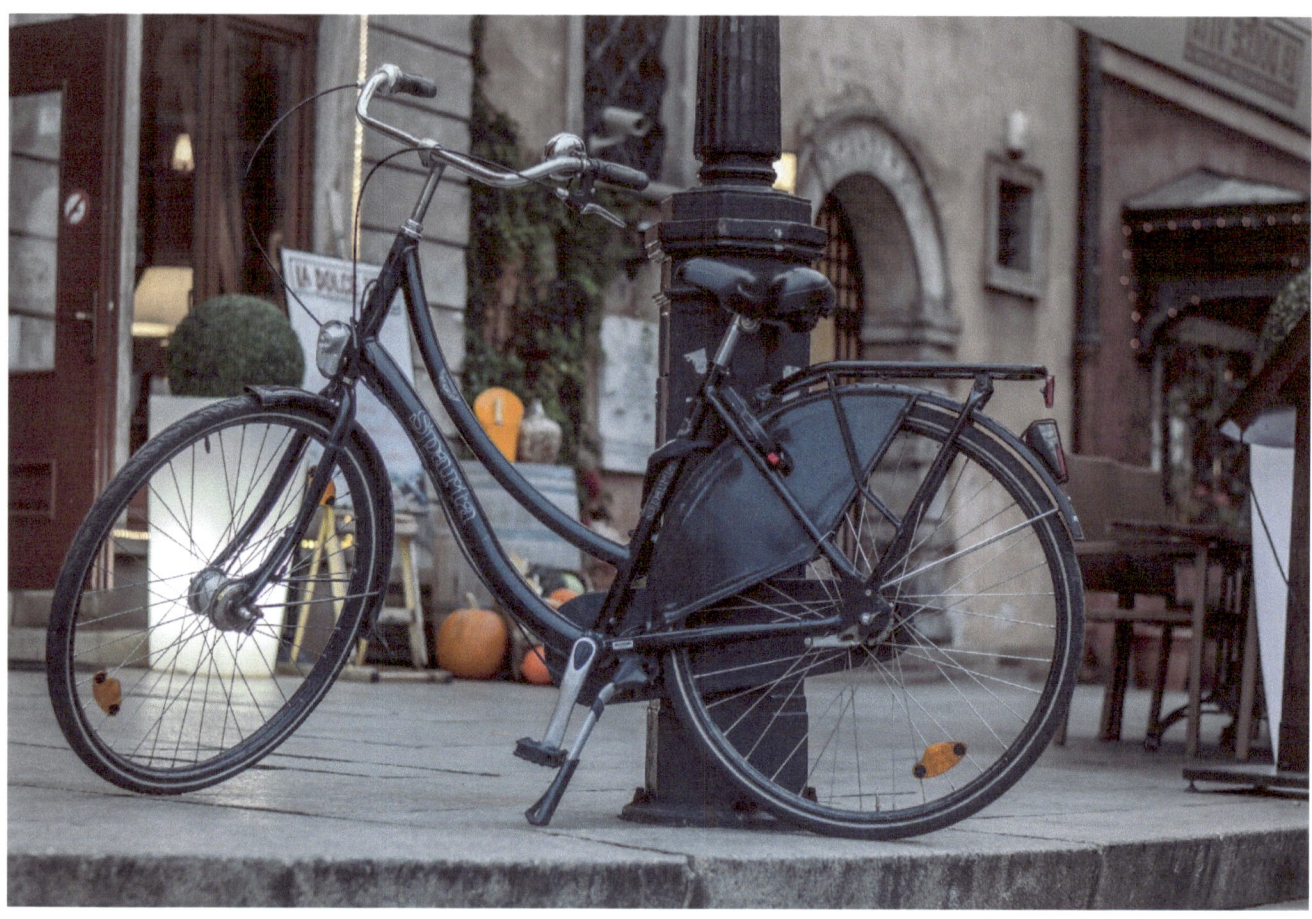

#Seen in Warsaw

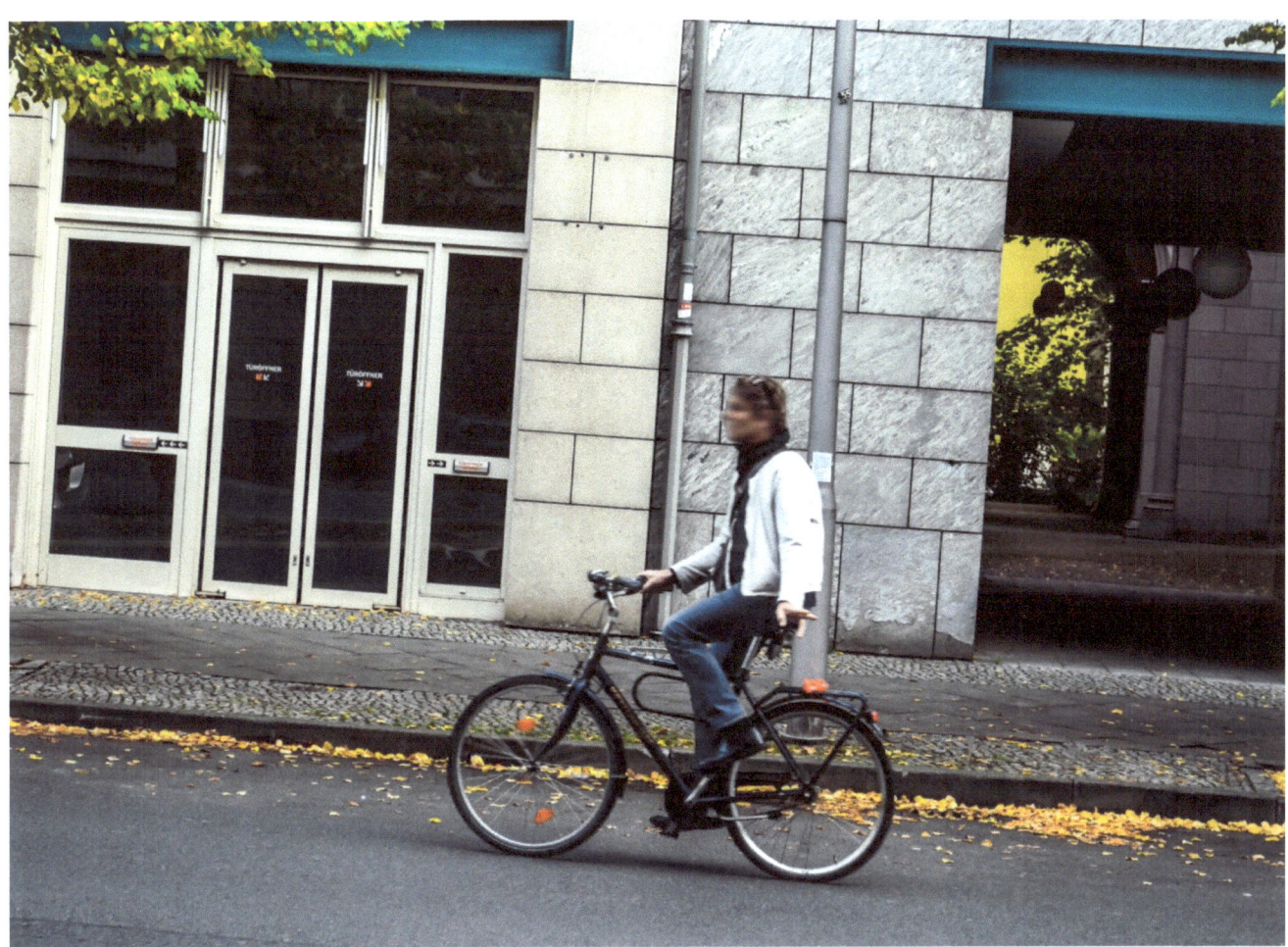

#Seen in Berlin

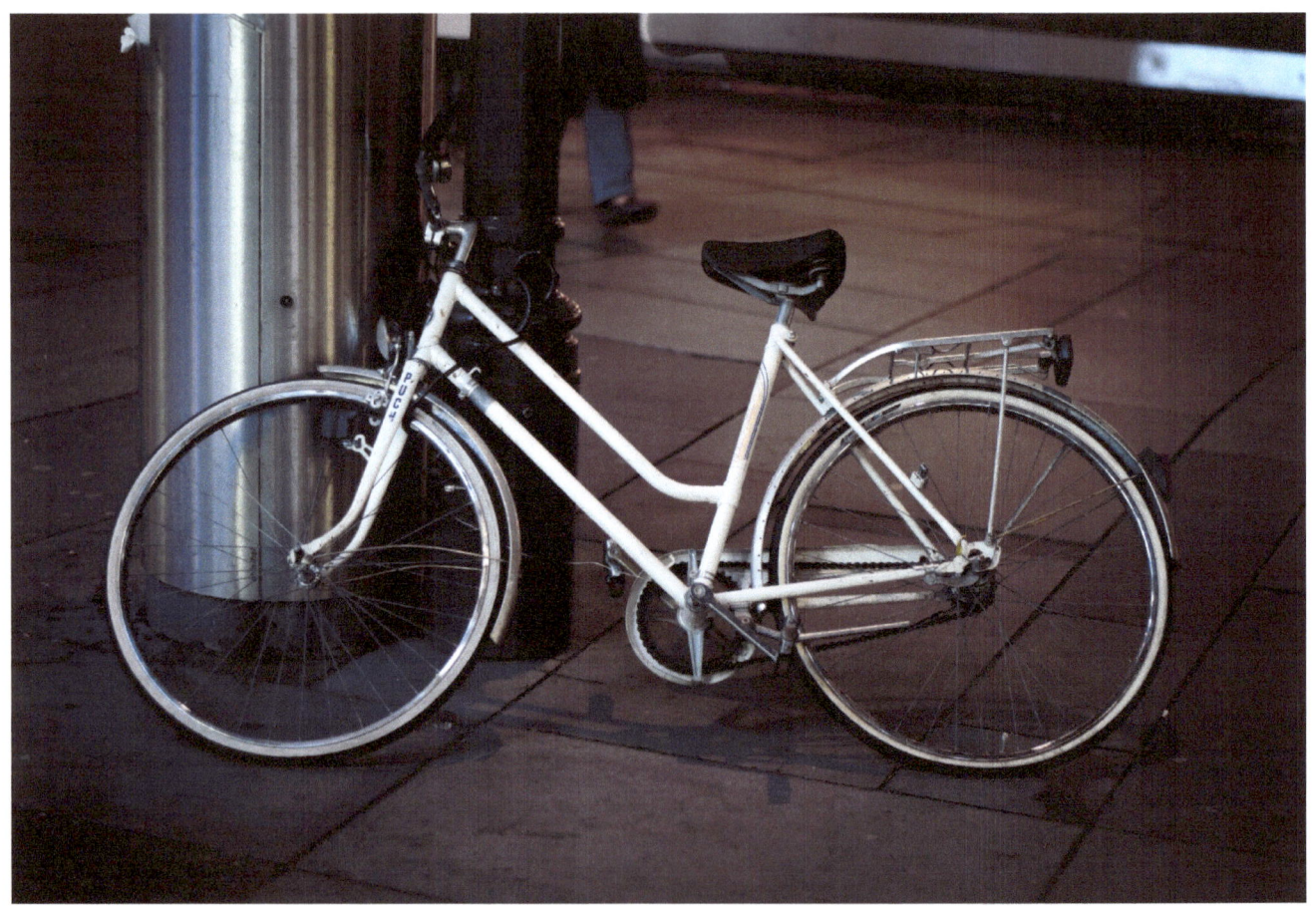

#Seen in Vienna

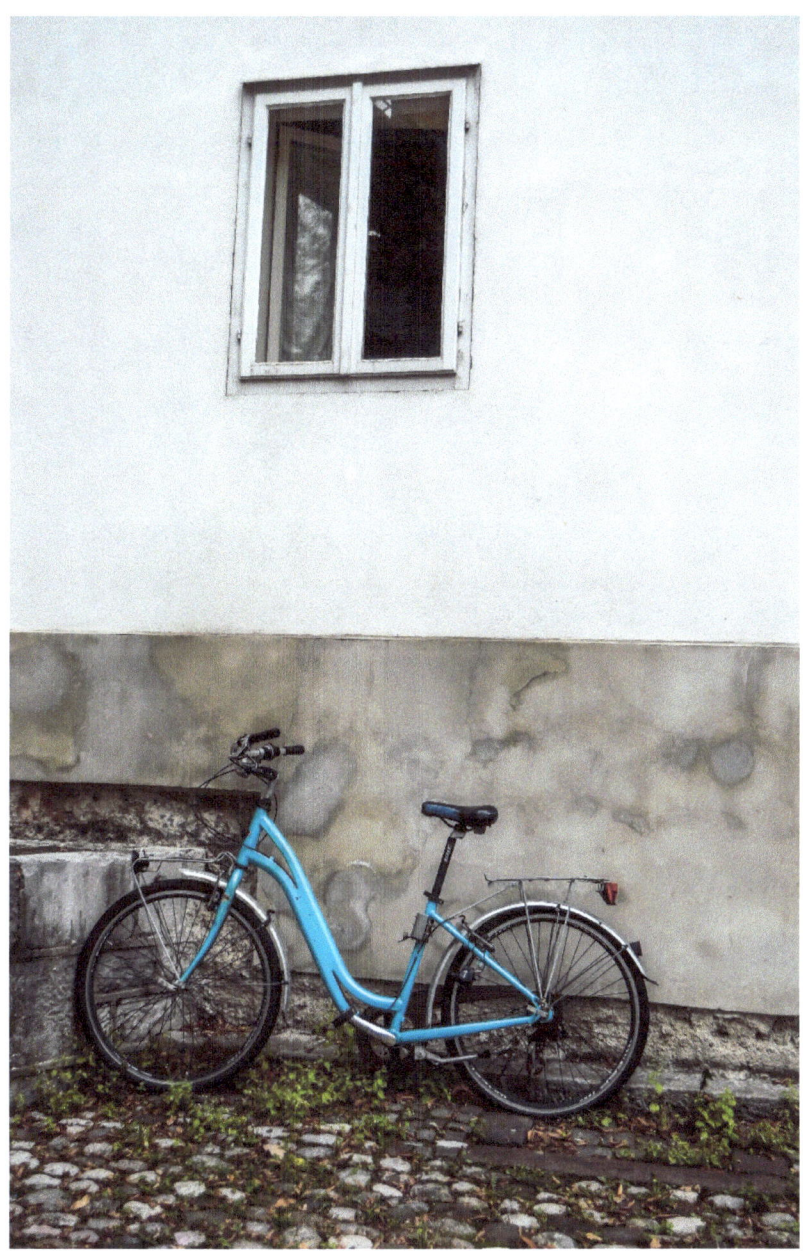

#Seen in Ljubljana

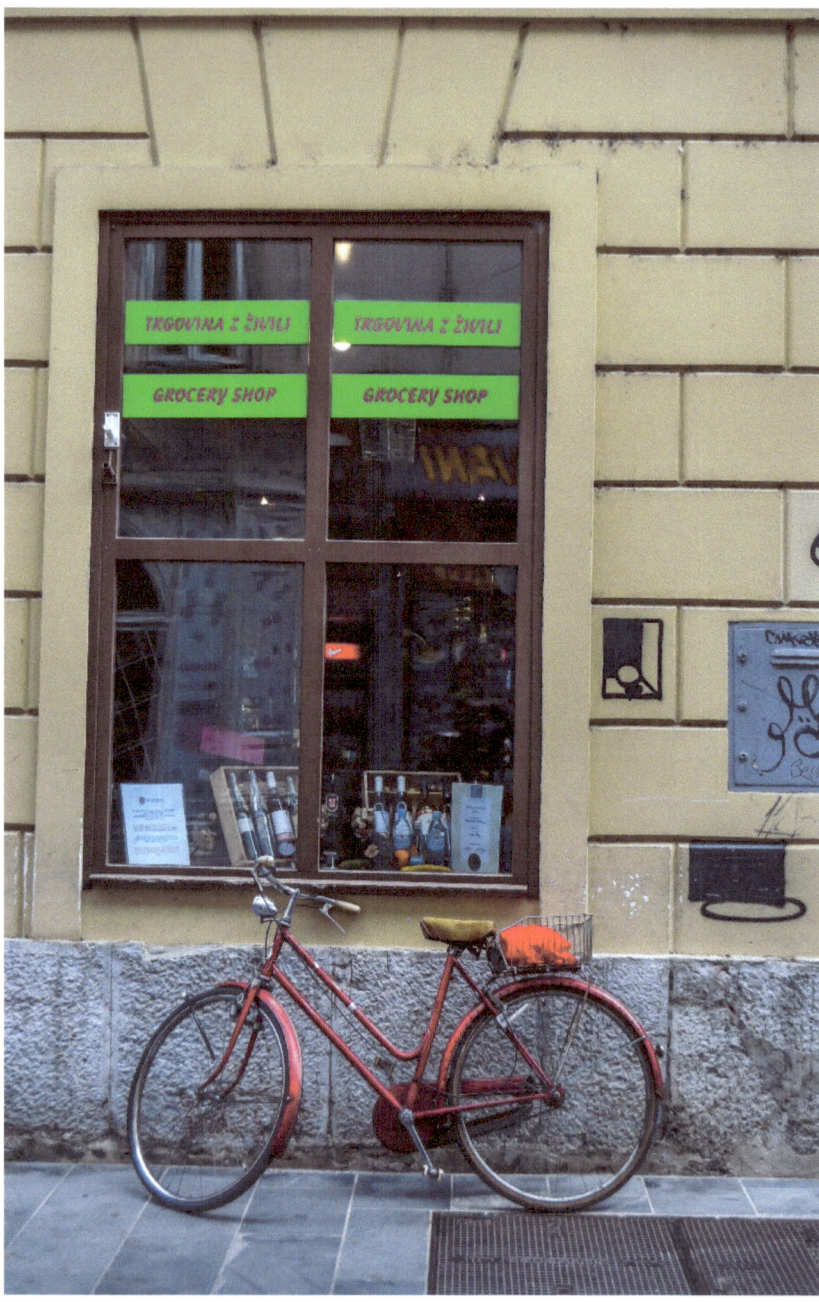

#Seen in Ljubljana

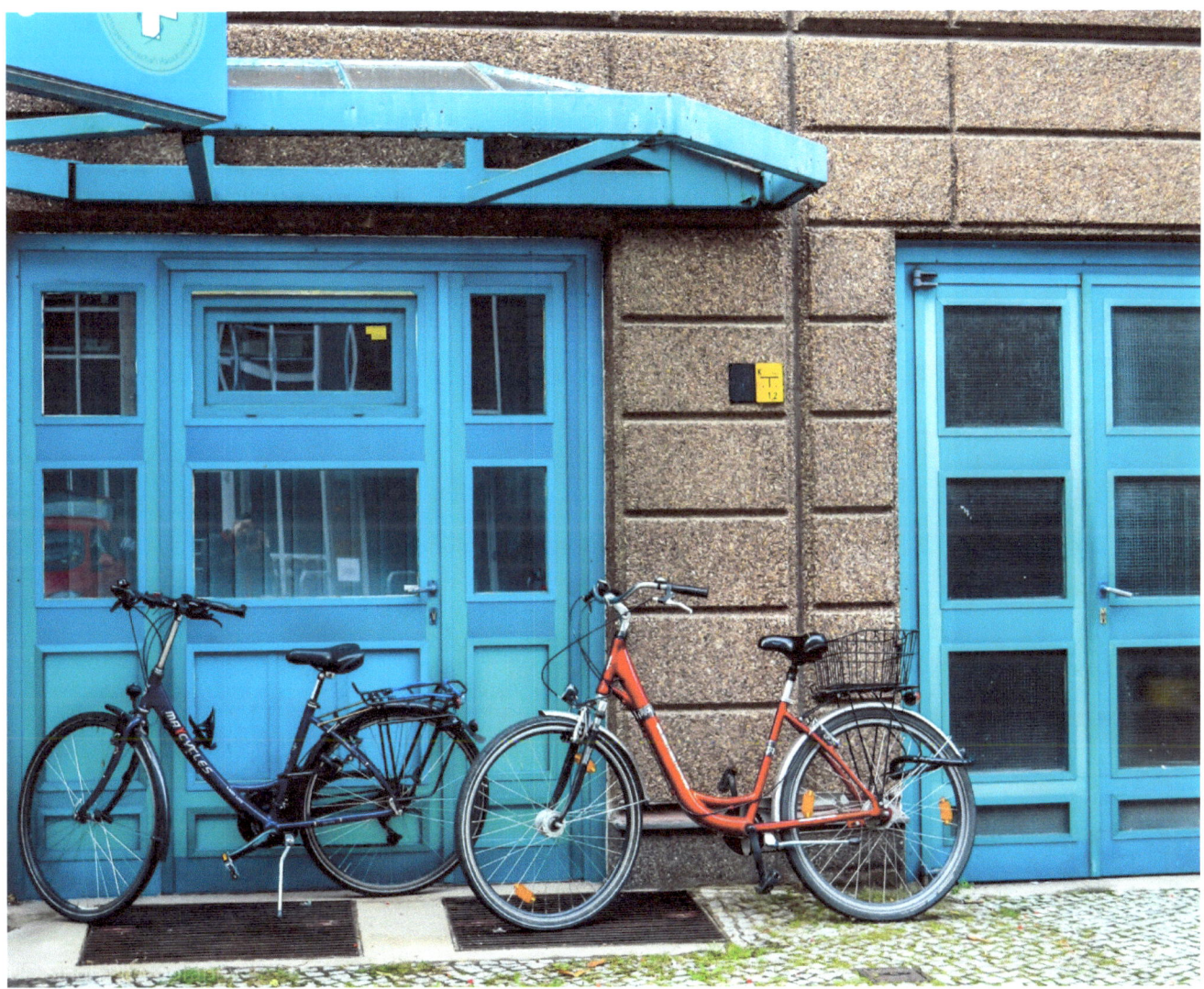

#Seen in Berlin

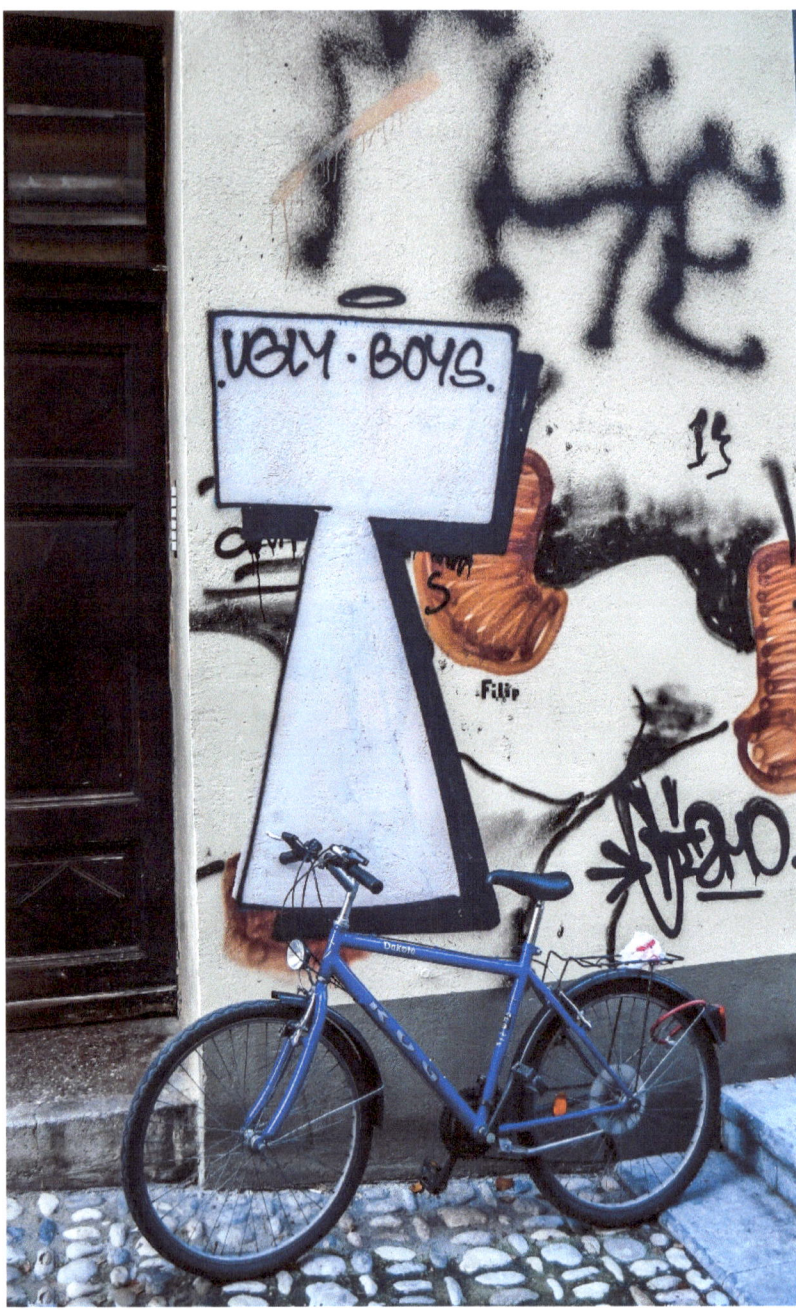

#Seen in Ljubljana

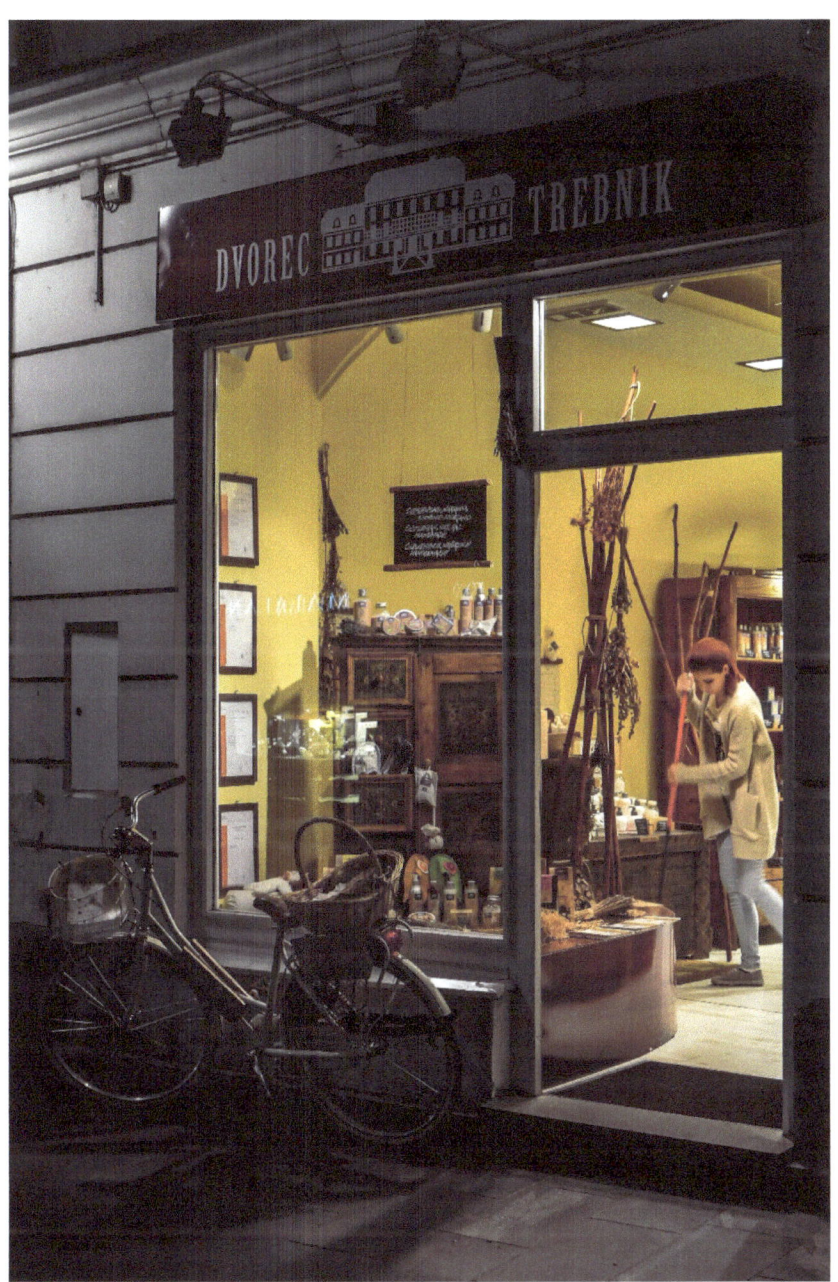

#Seen in Ljubljana

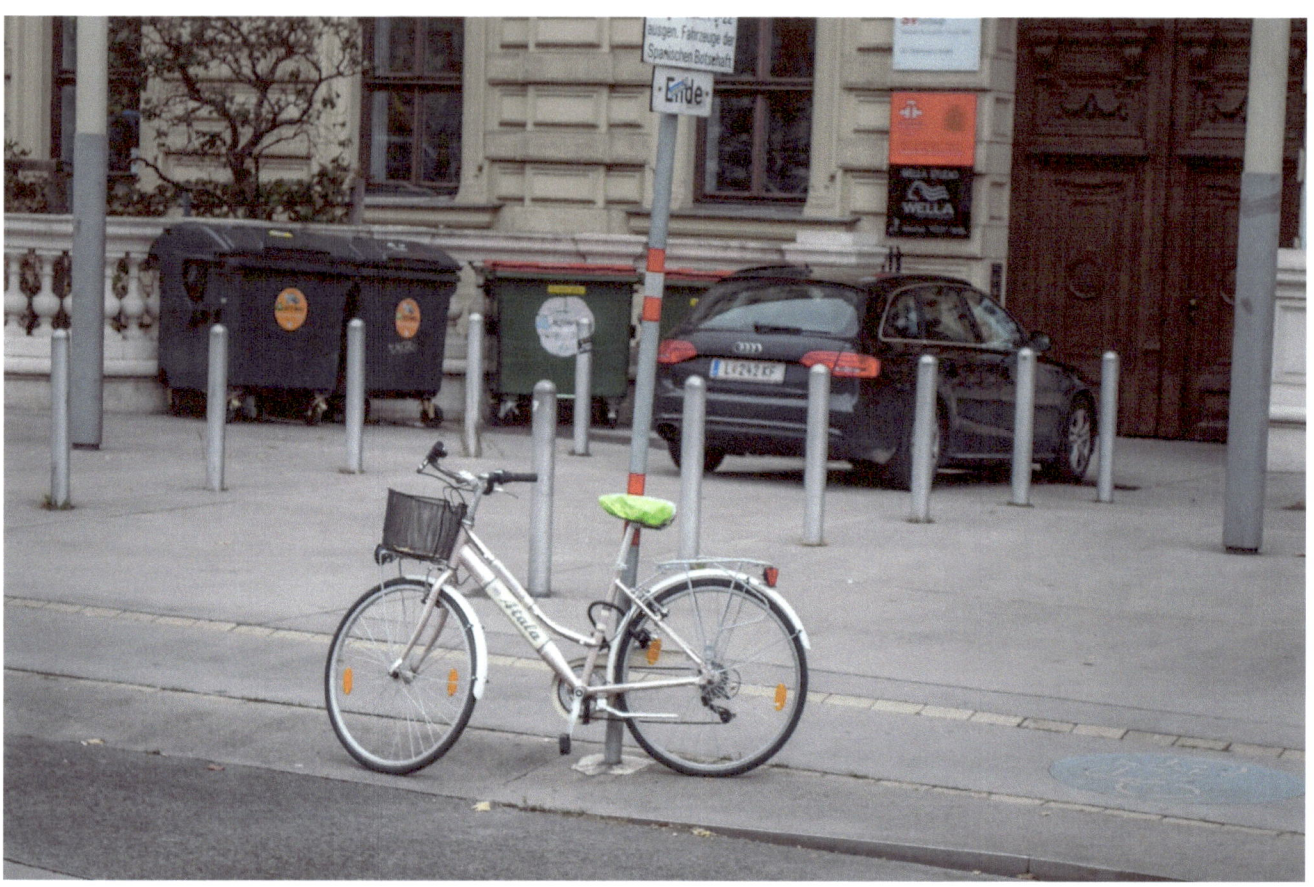

#Seen in Vienna

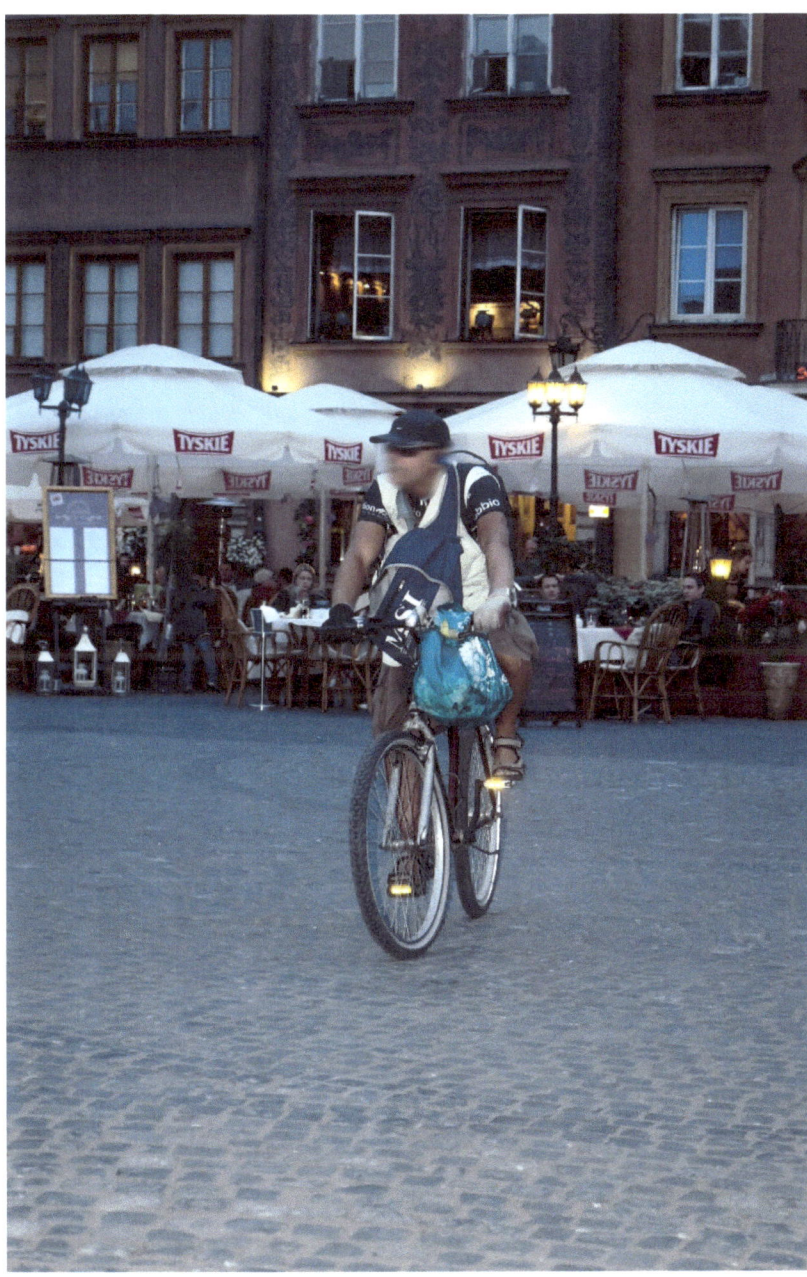

#Seen in Warsaw

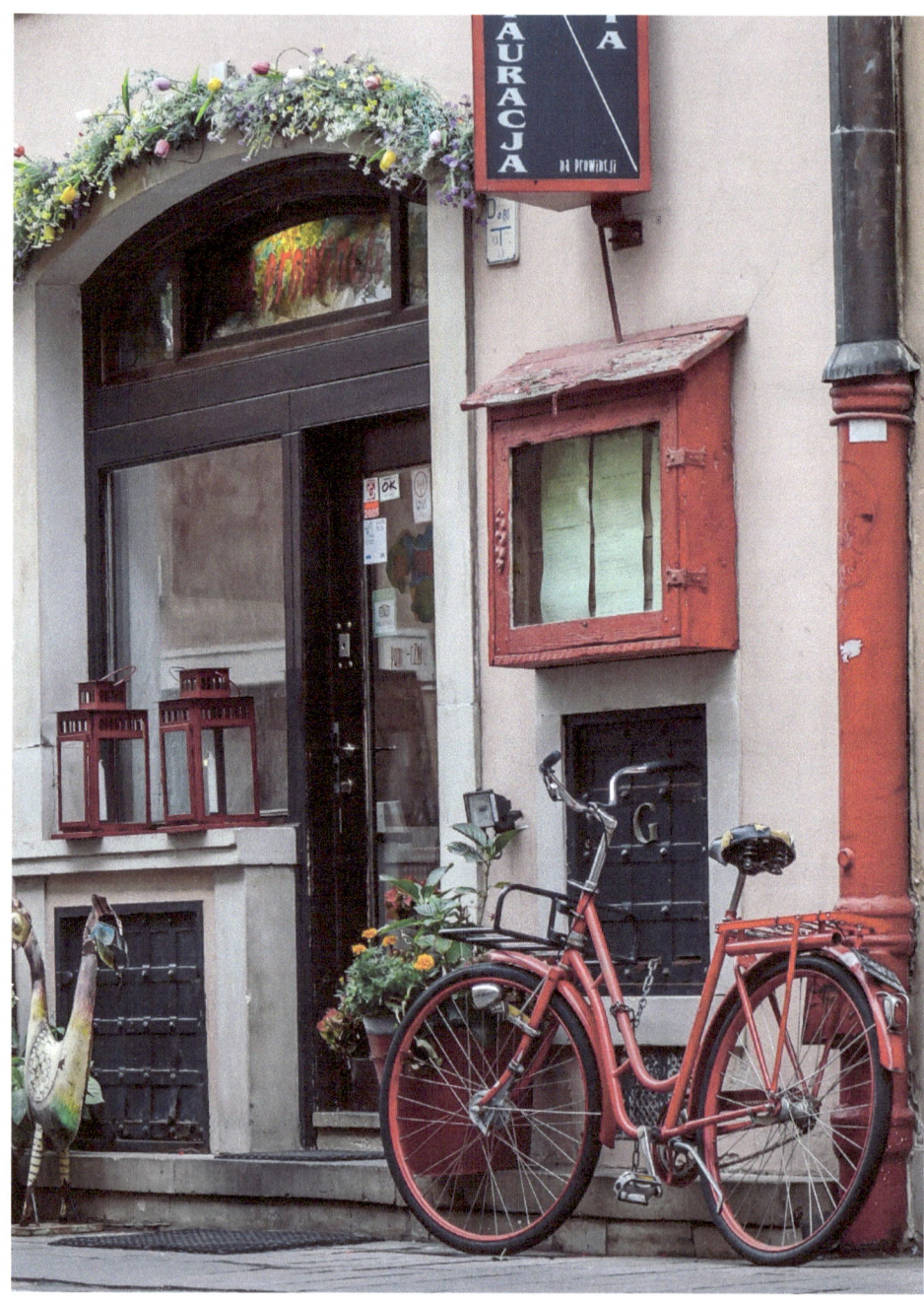

#Seen in Bratislava

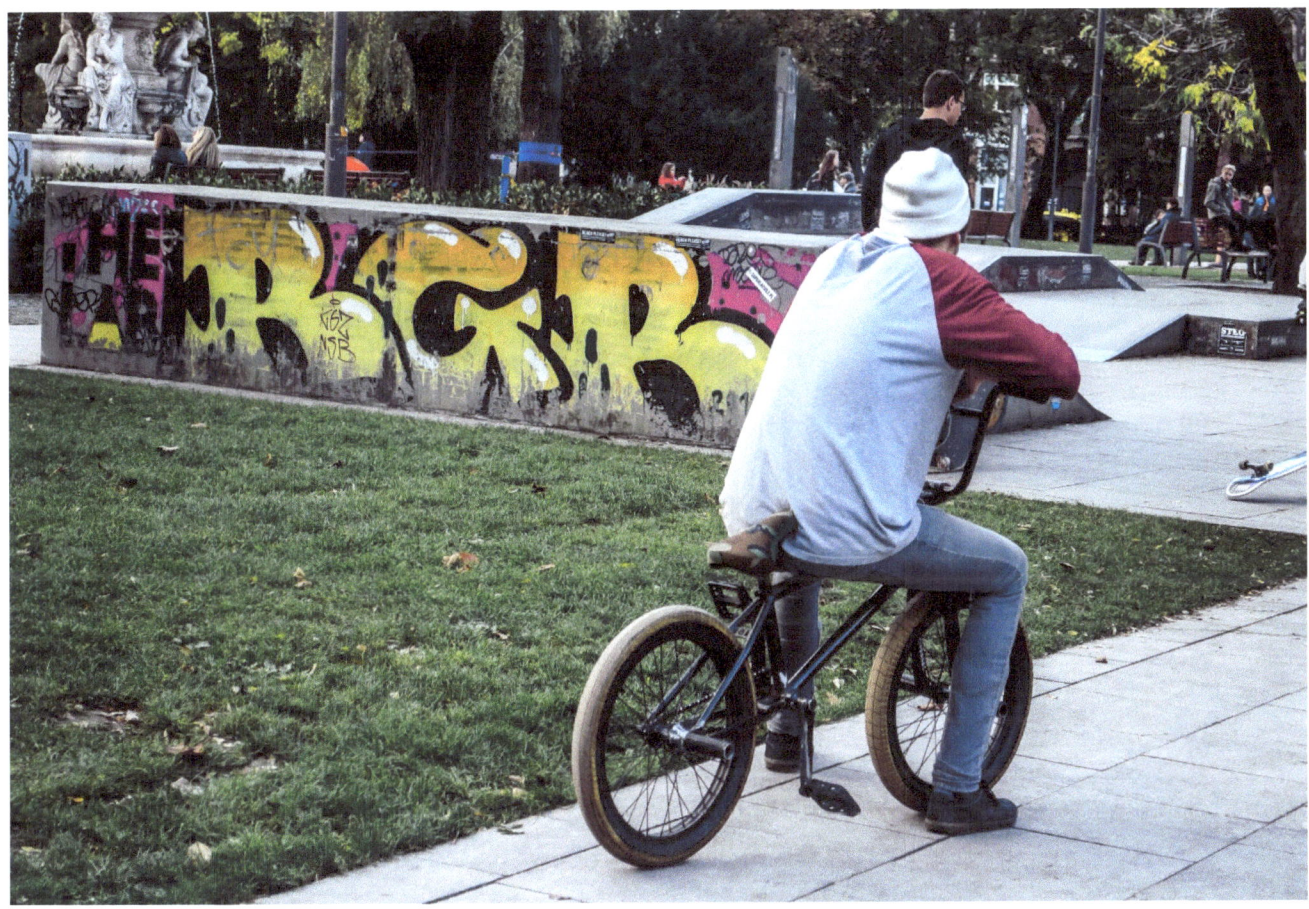

#Seen in Budapest

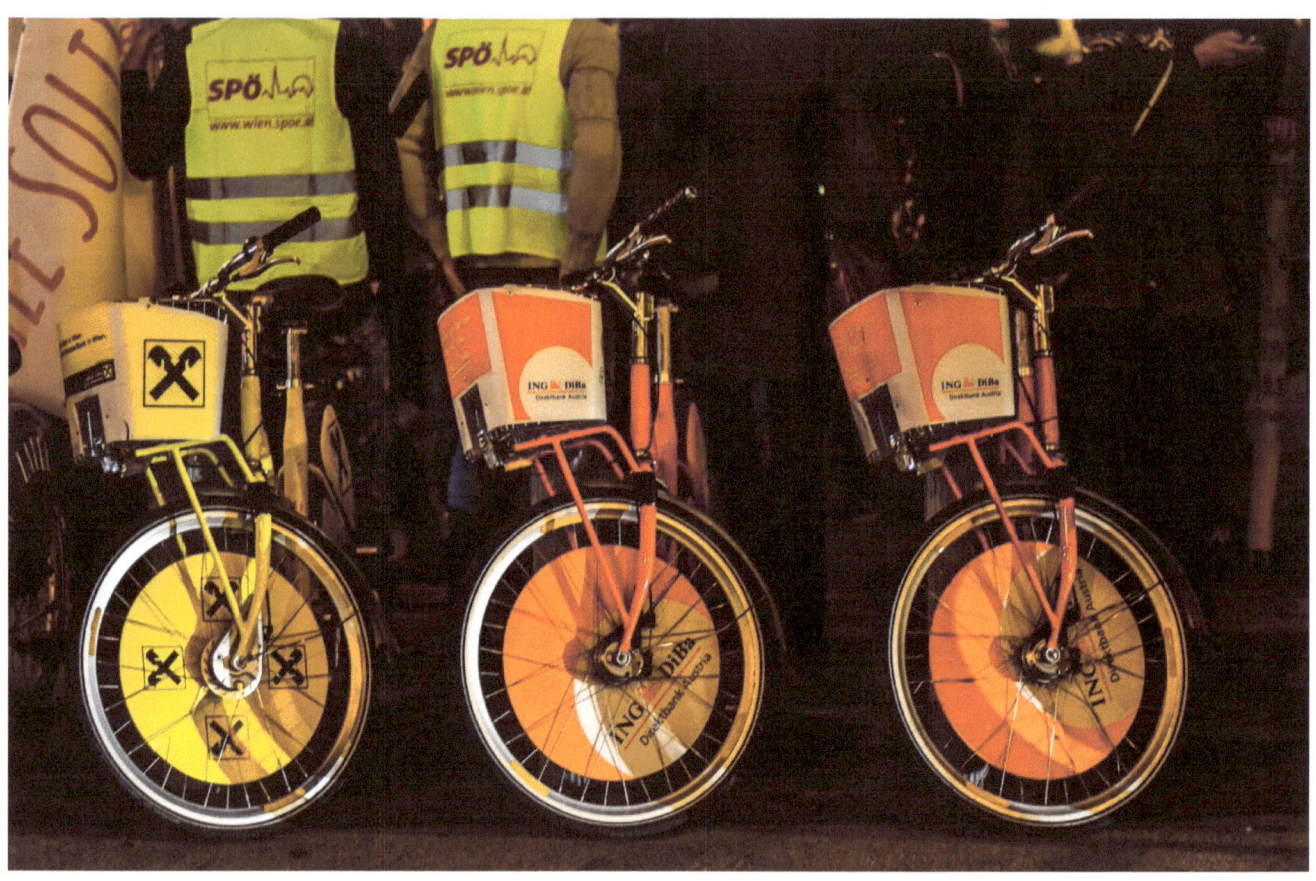

#Seen in Vienna

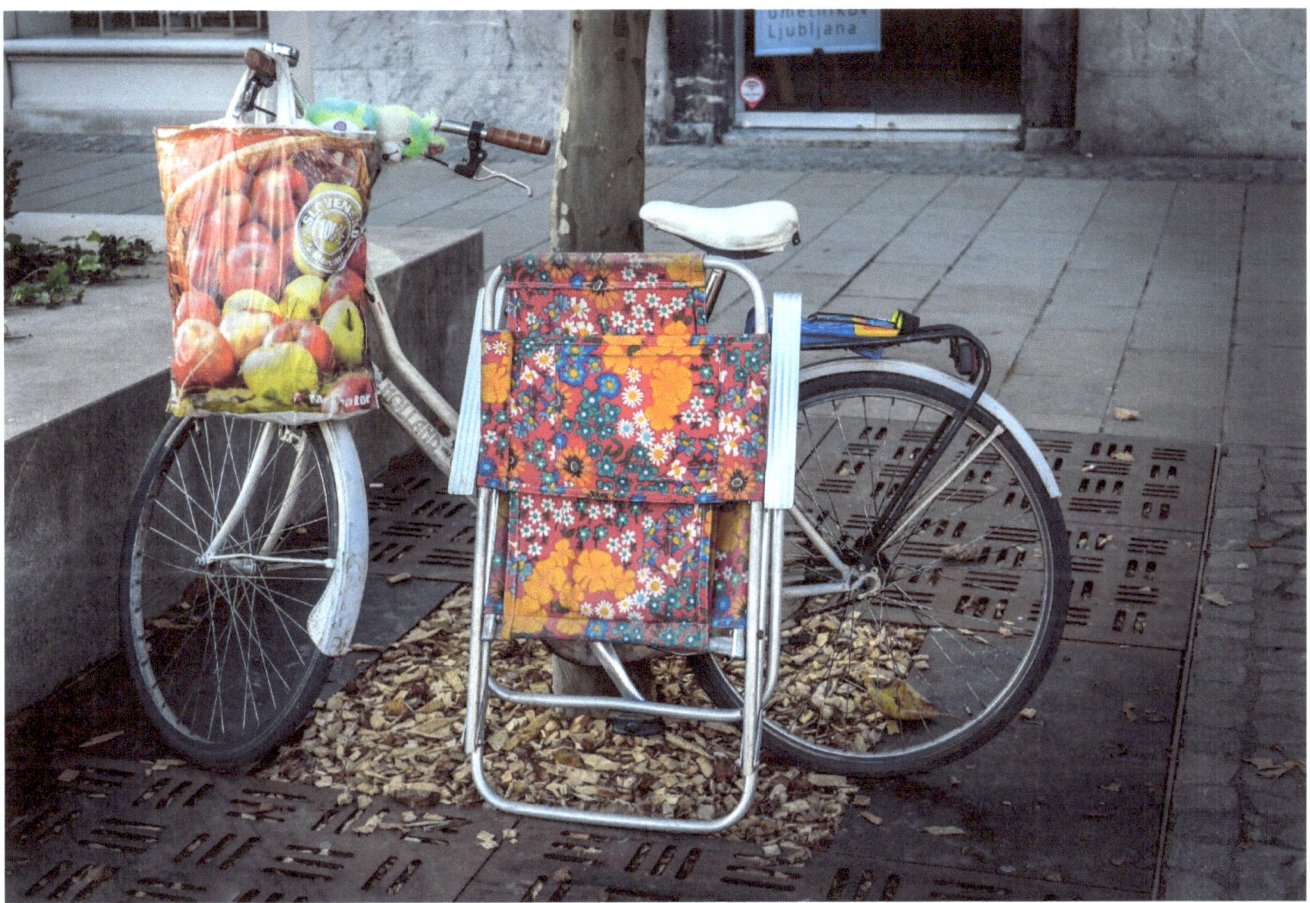

#Seen in Ljubljana

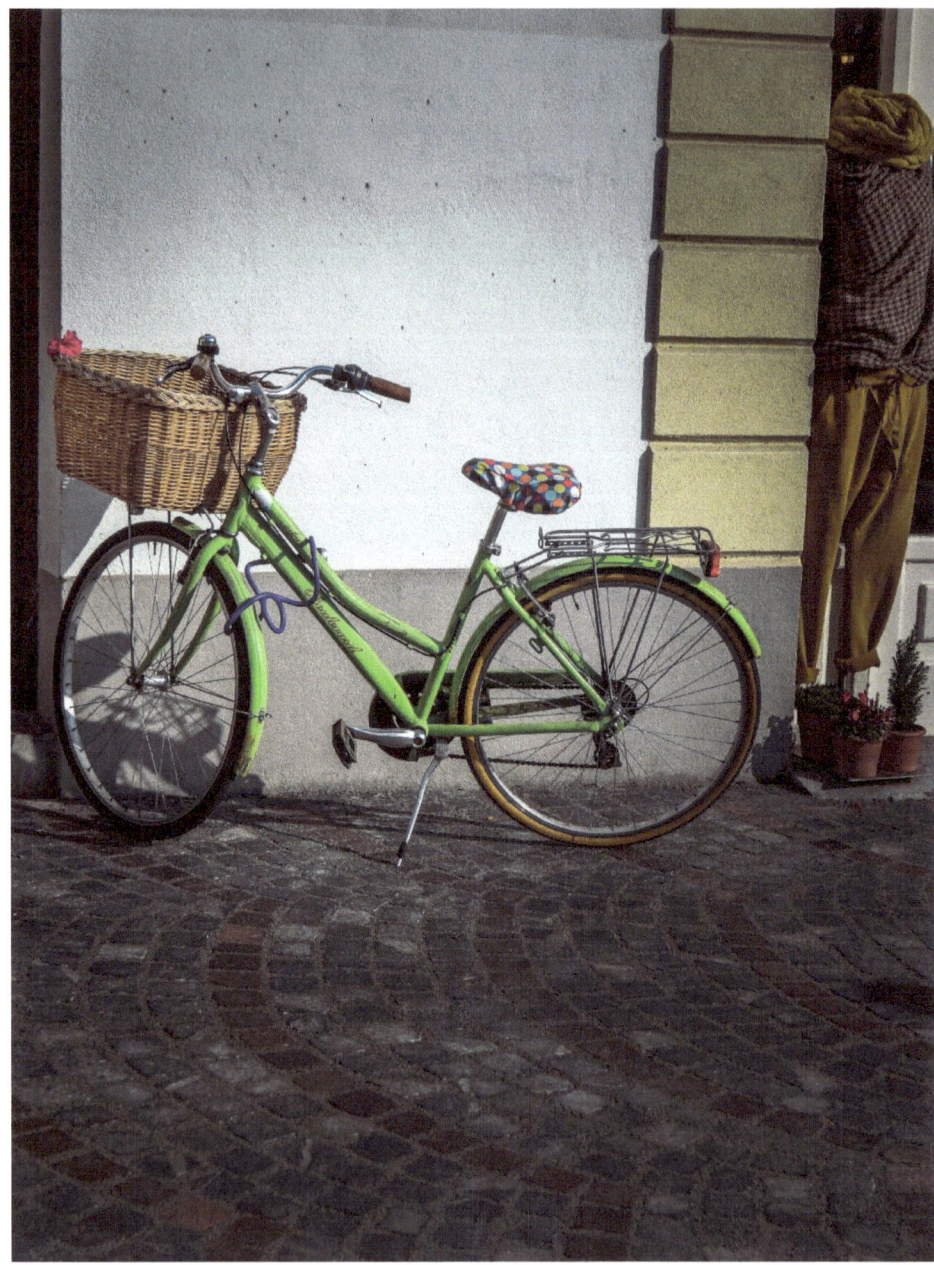

#Seen in Ljubljana

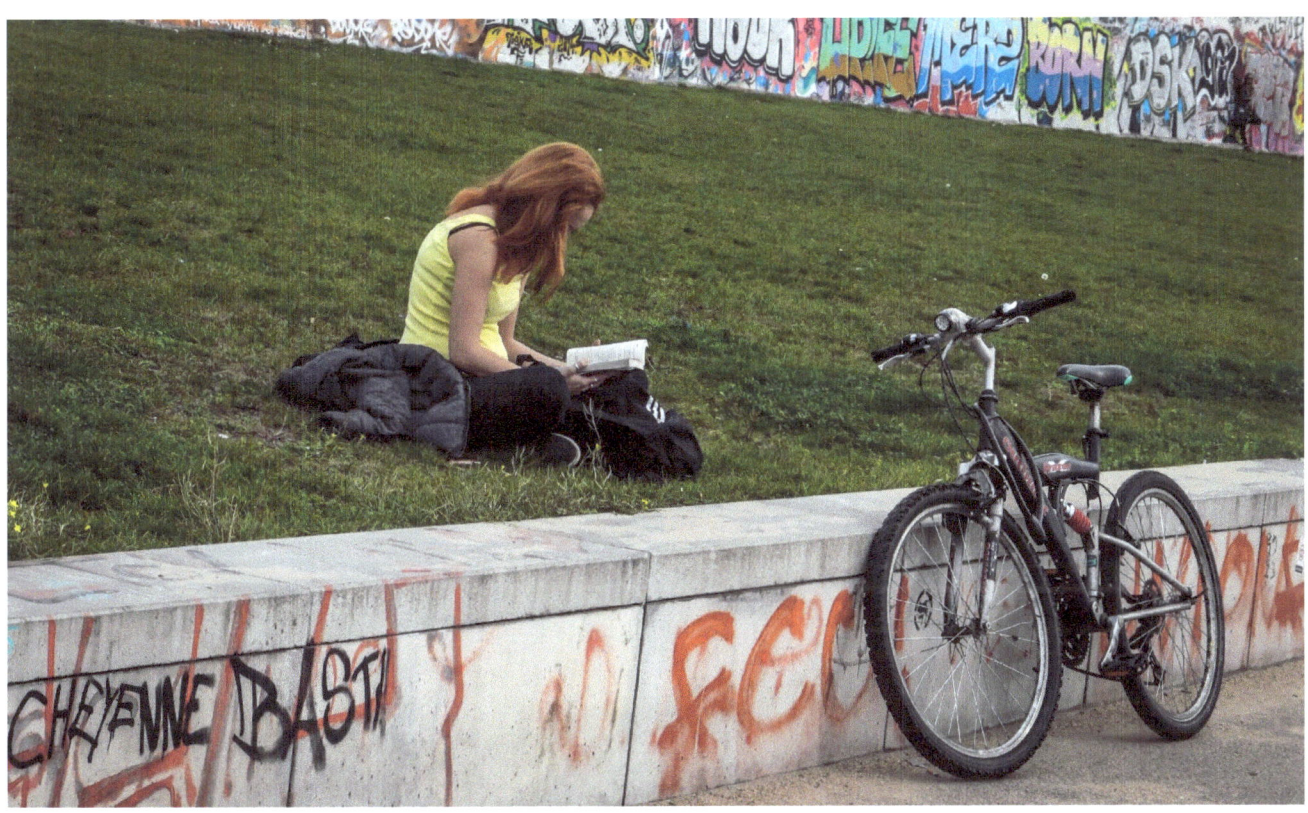

#Seen in Berlin

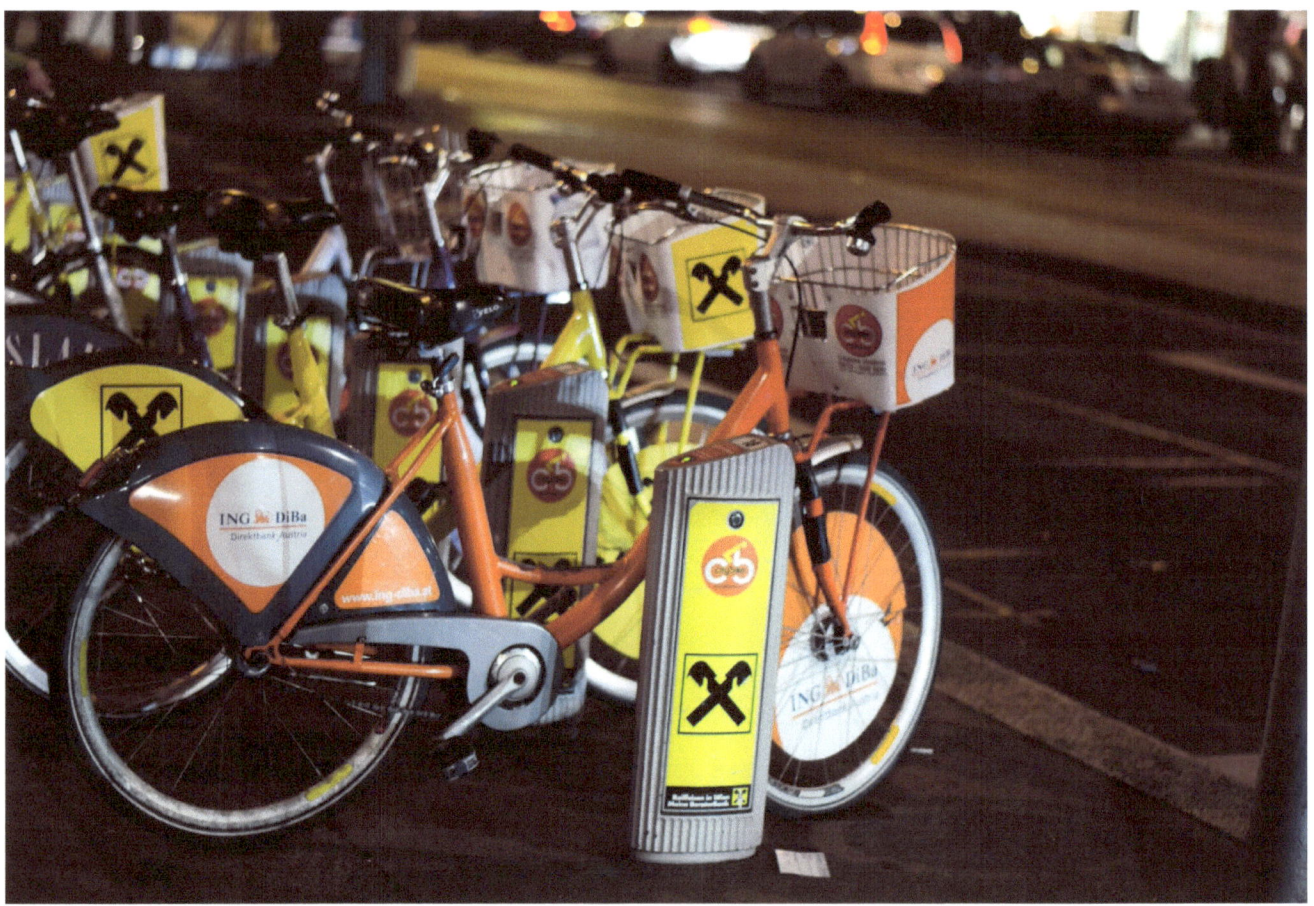

#Seen in Vienna

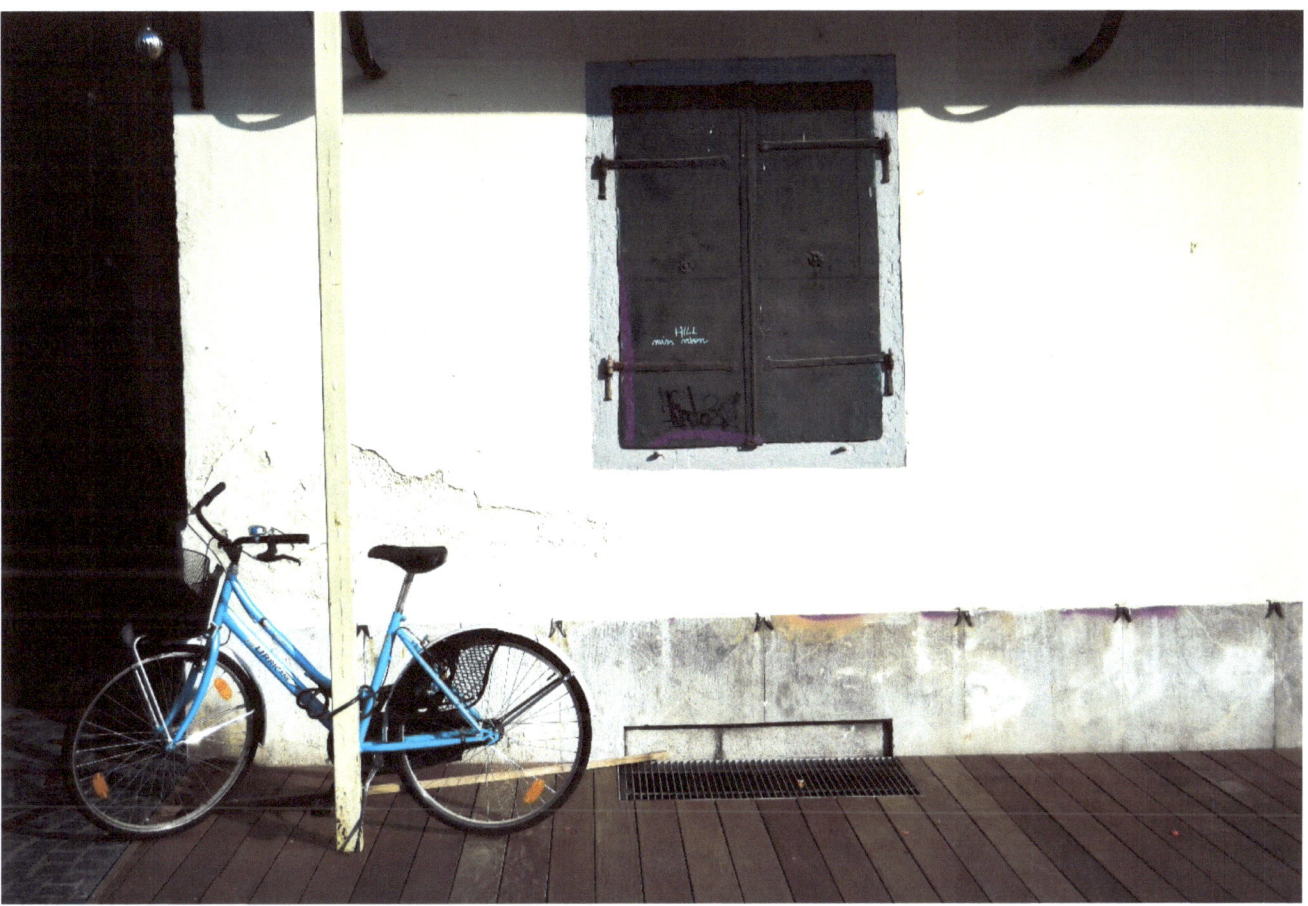

#Seen in Ljubljana

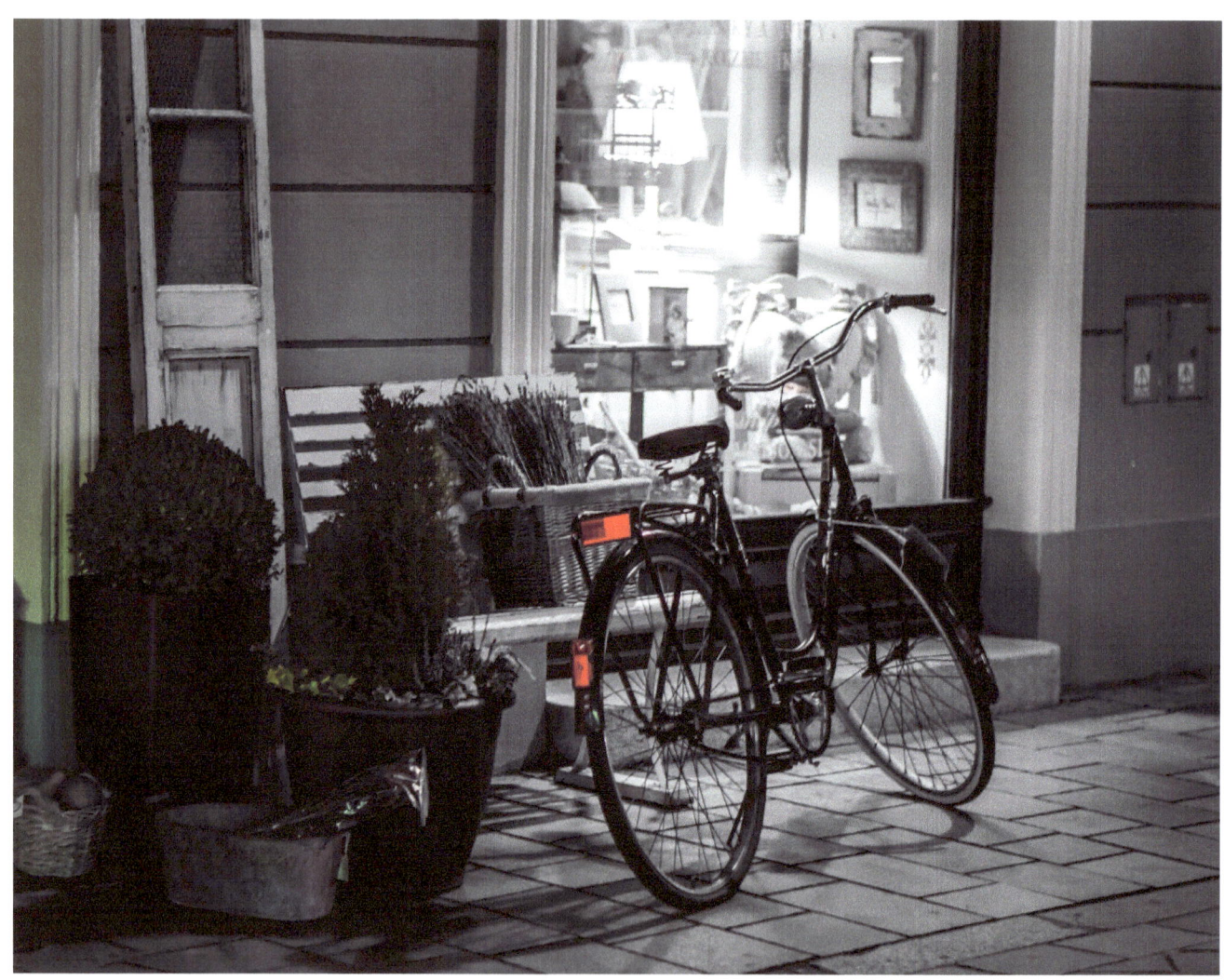

#Seen in Ljubljana

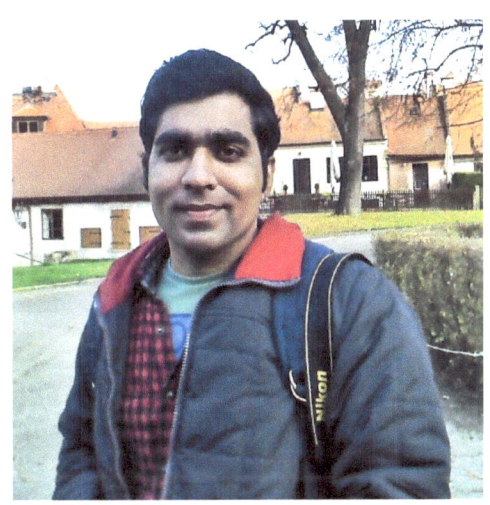

Udaybhan Singh is a Computer Engineer and a Management graduate born and educated in India. He loves business, philosophy, reading, blogging, music, art, travelling, cheese burst Pizza and Photography totally. When he is not seen working he is either watching sitcoms or learning guitar or reading a book or dreaming his next trip. This is his second published book on photographic art work. He has also authored a photographic art book titled 'Windows and Doors of Europe'.

He also runs a portal named **www.whitepuppie.com**. whitepuppie.com is a curated handpicked collection of global arts, handicrafts, exclusive lifestyle products and classy artifacts that empower rural artists and serves as a platform for established designers to showcase their exclusive work.

He is reachable on
https://udsinghprojects.wordpress.com or
Gmail : udsinghphotography@gmail.com
Instagram : udsingh

www.ingramcontent.com/pod-product-compliance
Lightning Source LLC
Chambersburg PA
CBHW050854180526
45159CB00007B/2676